KU-511-482

The Open University
Mathematics:
A Second Level Course

M205
Fundamentals of Computing

Block IV

Data Structures

Unit 2 Sequences: Static Storage

Unit 3 Sequences: Dynamic Storage

Prepared by the Course Team

The Open University

Course Team

Alan Best
Gordon Davies (*Chairman*)
Adam Gawronski (*ACS*)
Benedict Heal (*Academic Editor*)
Peter Leadbetter
John Newton
Jenny Preece (*Academic Editor*)
Hugh Robinson (*Academic Editor*)
Dave Sargent
David Saunders (*BBC*)
Eleanor Smith
Pete Thomas
Mike Williams (*Course Manager*)

Consultants

Jonathan Blandon
John Bramwell
Charles Easteal
Frank Lovis

External Assessor

Professor P A Samet (*University College, London*)

With assistance from:

Jonathan Davies (*Design*)
David Douglas (*Publishing Editor*)
Alison George (*Design*)
Richard Housden (*Maths*)
Diane Mole (*Design*)
M252 Tutors

The Open University, Walton Hall,
Milton Keynes.

First published 1988. Reprinted 1989, 1990, 1991, 1992, 1993, 1994.

Copyright © 1988 The Open University.

All rights reserved. No part of this work may be
reproduced, stored in a retrieval system or transmitted,
in any form or by any means, without written
permission from the publisher.

Printed and bound in the United Kingdom by
Staples Printers Rochester Limited,
Neptune Close, Medway City Estate, Frindsbury,
Rochester, Kent ME2 4LT.

ISBN 0 335 14331 8

This text forms part of the correspondence element of
an Open University Second Level Course.

For general availability of supporting material referred
to in this text, please write to Open University
Educational Enterprises Limited, 12 Cofferidge Close,
Stony Stratford, Milton Keynes, MK11 1BY,
Great Britain.

Further information on Open University courses may
be obtained from The Admissions Office, The Open
University, P.O. Box 48, Walton Hall, Milton Keynes
MK7 6AB.

Unit 2 Sequences: Static Storage

Prepared by the Course Team

Contents

Study guide

In the previous unit we described the specification and implementation of a number of structured data types: *arrays*, *records* and *tables*. We described these data structures as *static* structures in the sense that their size was predefined, that is, the number of elements and the amount of storage required to hold these elements was fixed; they cannot change as a result of operations on the data structures.

We noted that not all data structures were static. You will meet a number of data structures whose size (number of elements) may vary as a result of operations on the data. Such structures are called **dynamic data structures**. For example, in a word processing system, the insertion or deletion of words in a piece of text will increase or decrease the length of the text and so change the amount of storage required to hold it. It is impossible in such applications to determine the precise storage requirements before program execution commences. You are already familiar with character strings and some of the operations on them, which are fundamental to text processing. One of the most important attributes of a string is the variability of its length under operations such as insertion, deletion and concatenation (the joining of two strings). A string is one example of a **sequence**.

In this and the next unit we consider the abstract data type called a **sequence**, and operations on sequences. We also consider some sequences, namely **stacks** and **queues**, on which only a limited range of operations is allowed. The description of these data structures follows the pattern established in *Unit 1* of this block: first we describe each data structure in terms of *what* operations may be applied to it and then we describe *how* the data structure could be implemented in Pascal. Two essentially different methods of implementation are considered; in this unit *contiguous* storage representations are described. These involve the representation of a dynamic data structure using a static storage structure and we consider the constraints imposed by this method. In the next unit a more flexible, dynamic organization of storage is considered together with the storage management procedures necessary to support it.

After studying this unit you should understand what a sequence is and the operations that are performed on sequences (listed on p.6). You should also have a detailed understanding of two specific types of sequences; stacks and queues. Your knowledge should be sufficient for you to describe the data structures abstractly and also how they are represented and implemented in Pascal.

The introduction is short; it defines a sequence.

Section 2 is a little longer, but should take less than an evening to study. It describes the operations that can be performed on a general sequence.

Section 3 deals with representations of a sequence. It is quite a long theoretical section and will probably need more than one evening to study.

Section 4 is about stacks. It should only take an evening to study the theory but there is also a practical exercise, so allow one and a half evenings.

Section 5 is a long section with theory and a substantial practical exercise. You will probably need at least two evenings to complete all of it.

Section 6 is the summary, which only requires a few minutes to read.

Study plan

Section		Media required	Time
1	Introduction	Text	
2	Operations on sequences	Text	2 evenings
3	Representation of a sequence	Text	
4	Stacks	Text HCF	1½ evenings
5	Queues	Text HCF	2½ evenings
	Summary	Text	

1 Introduction: Specification of a sequence

In *Block I* we introduced the concept of a sequence. Our definition was:

a sequence is a data structure in which zero or more items of data of a predefined type are placed one after another in an order determined by some predefined relationship.

In other words, a sequence is an ordered collection of *zero or more items of a predefined type*. The sequence is almost certainly the most common data structure, and a substantial proportion of the total time spent in data-processing applications involves operations on sequences of data. Many of these sequences are very long – for example, the list of products sold by a supermarket chain, the list of spare parts held by a motor manufacturer, or the details of the policy holders of an insurance company. Such sequences are frequently so long that they cannot be held in the working store of a computer and must be placed in its backing storage. In this case, the sequence is called a **file** and will be processed by means of the **file-processing** techniques described in *Block V* of this course. In this unit we shall look in detail at shorter sequences, which can be held in working store, and shall see how a range of operations can be performed on them.

Exercise 1.1

Consider the definition of a sequence given above and the definition of a one-dimensional array as given in *Unit 1* of *Block II*. What is the essential difference between a sequence and a one-dimensional array?

2 *Operations on sequences*

We identify some basic operations which are associated with a sequence:

- Creation and initialization of a sequence (initially empty).
- Selection and retrieval of a specified item from a sequence.
- Insertion of an item in a sequence.
- Deletion of a specified item from a sequence.
- Rearranging the items of a sequence.
- Updating a specified item in a sequence (by assignment).
- Interrogating the size (number of items) of a sequence, in particular testing for an empty sequence.

Although introduced here in association with the data structure sequence, these operations are equally applicable to all *dynamic* data structures.

As an illustrative example of a sequence and operations on a sequence, we shall take a computer system which maintains a list of the flights due to arrive at an airport and provides facilities to keep this list up to date as new flights are added and existing flights are cancelled, delayed, or otherwise amended. The system must also provide answers to requests for flight information. The current list of flights is held in the working store of the computer as a sequence of records, each record having a *time* field (numeric) and a *source* field (string) as shown in Figure 2.1. The flights are held in chronological order of due arrival times. The field used for ordering a sequence is called a **key field**; thus in the flight records, the *time* field is the key field and the *source* field is a **non-key field**. We shall assume that the *field* values are *unique*,

time	source
16.00	Manchester
17.05	Glasgow
17.30	Belfast
17.45	Dublin
18.00	Bristol

Figure 2.1 *A sequence of flight records*

that is, no two flights have the same actual arrival time and no two flights are from the same source. This may not be very realistic but it will simplify our programs and allow us to concentrate on the main features of a sequence.

We shall refer to Figure 2.1 time and time again in the following sections. You may wish to write out a copy of it for easy reference.

2.1 Creation and initialization

A wide range of operations can be associated with a sequence but before we can apply any of them the sequence must exist. We therefore, introduce the idea of *creation* of a sequence which initially has no elements. Precisely what this involves will become clear soon, when we consider the representation of a sequence. For now you may think of creation, in the programming sense, as defining or declaring a data structure. *Initialization* is the process of preparing that structure for use; this is analogous to the familiar process of initializing a variable.

2.2 Retrieval

We next examine some operations associated with the retrieval of data from a sequence into which a number of items have already been inserted. Before data can be retrieved we must establish that it is present in the sequence; this involves *searching*. Searching for data also raises the question of how to access an *individual item* in a sequence. A fundamental attribute of a sequence is the *order* of its elements. We said in our definition that the items in a sequence are placed one after another in an order determined by some predefined relationship. In the example of flights due at an airport in Figure 2.1, the ordering is chronological. Only the first item can be accessed directly. Access to an item other than the first involves access to the preceding item. (This is the *only* information we have about the position of an item in the sequence.) Thus, access to a required item generally involves a sequential search of the sequence, starting with the first item and examining each successive item in turn until *either* the required item is found or it is determined that the required item is not present in the sequence.

In our airport example there are two different situations to be considered:

- Retrieval of data from a *non-key field*, given the value in the corresponding *key field*; for example, What is the source of the flight due to arrive at 17.45?
- Retrieval of data from a *key field*, given the value in the corresponding *non-key field*; for example, What time is the next flight from Belfast due to arrive?

We look first at retrieval of data from a *non-key field* given the value in the corresponding *key field*. Suppose we are asked to find the source of the flight due at 17.45. Clearly, we have to search through the elements of the sequence examining the entry in the *time* field of each element and, in doing so, we use the fact that the values in the *time* field are ordered. The process works as shown in the design in Figure 2.2.

Note that, since a sequence may be empty, we must test first to see if there are any items to be searched before we commence the search process. (This is referred to as *safe* programming.) As you have seen in *Block II*, the result of a search must be *either* an item *or* a report that the required item is not found.

Notice also that, on exit from this searching process:

- If the sequence is exhausted then the required data is *not* present.
- Else if the *time* field of the current item *equals* the required item, then the *source* field value *has been* retrieved.
- Else if the current *time* field is *greater* than the required time, then the required data is *not* present.

When we consider the representation of a sequence, you will see that it may be possible to simplify this process as we did when searching the elements of an array in *Unit 2* of *Block II*.

Now we look at retrieval of data from a *key field* given the value in the corresponding *non-key field*. In this case we cannot take

```
1   if the sequence is empty
2   then
3       write out 'no data items present'
4   else
5       get first item from beginning of sequence
6       loop while sequence is not exhausted and time of current
               item  <  required time
7           move to next item
8       loopend
9       if sequence is exhausted
10      then
11          write out 'item required is not present'
12      else
13          if current time field greater than required time field
14          then
15              write out 'required item is not present'
16          else
17              retrieve source of current item
18          ifend
19      ifend
20  ifend
```

Figure 2.2 *A design to search for and retrieve data from a non-key field*

```
1   if the sequence is empty
2   then
3       write out 'no data items present'
4   else
5       get first item from beginning of sequence
6       loop while sequence not exhausted and source of current
               item  < >  required source
7           move to next item
8       loopend
9       if sequence is exhausted
10      then
11          write out 'required item is not present'
12      else
13          retrieve time of current item
14      ifend
15  ifend
```

Figure 2.3 *Retrieval of data from a key field*

advantage of the order of the items. The search process works as shown in the design in Figure 2.3.

The essential difference between this process and that in Figure 2.2 is the way in which it terminates when the search is not successful. A search for a specified value of a key field terminates on reaching the position in the sequence where that value would be located if present; a search for some non-key value must continue to the end of the sequence before we can determine the absence of the required data.

2.3 Insertion

When a new item is inserted in a sequence it must be put in at exactly the right place. In our example of flight arrivals this means inserting each new item so as to maintain the correct chronological order. If, for example (*17.15, Cardiff*) is to be inserted, it must go between (*17.05, Glasgow*) and (*17.30, Belfast*). This means that the sequence must first be searched on the *key field* to determine the right place to put the new item. A possible first design outline for the required process is shown in Figure 2.4.

```
1   start at the beginning of the sequence and
    get first item
2   loop while current key < given key and
            sequence is not exhausted
3       move to next item
4   loopend
5   insert given item before current item
6   increase the size of the sequence by one
```

Figure 2.4 *Insertion in a sequence – a first outline*

There are two points to note about this process:

(i) The searching process determines the item (*if any*) *before* which the new item is to be inserted.

(ii) The insertion process, as outlined in Figure 2.4, will not deal with insertion in an empty sequence or insertion at the end of the sequence, i.e. it only works if there is an item before which to make the insertion. Insertion at the end requires a special piece of program.

You might think that this minor complication could be overcome by first searching for an item *after* which to put the new item; but on reflection you will realize that insertion at the beginning of a sequence will then present a problem.

There are simple techniques to cope with these special cases which are more easily understood when we examine representations of a sequence. For the moment our purpose is to describe what is required rather than *how* it is achieved. The separation of these two aspects enables us to focus on one at a time – this is what abstraction is about.

SAQ 2.1 _____

1 Using the insertion process in Figure 2.4, show the steps involved in inserting the record

   30114   Soft brown sugar   49

into the sequence shown in Figure 2.5.

2 For the sequence of records shown in Figure 2.5

  (a) State which one of the three fields is the key field.

  (b) Write a top-level design (based on the one in either Figure 2.2 or Figure 2.3 as appropriate) to return from this sequence the number of cases of
     (i) stock item number 30115,
     (ii) soft brown sugar
  or report that the data is not present in the sequence.

Stock No.	Description	No. of cases
30110	Granulated sugar	95
30113	Icing sugar	27
30115	Caster sugar	35
30117	Demerara sugar	82

Figure 2.5

Solution 2.1

1 First locate the point at which the new record (with key field value 30114) must be inserted: start with the first item, stock number 30110.

The current key (30110) < given key (30114) and the sequence is not exhausted so move to the next item, stock number 30113

and repeat the loop.

The current key (30113) < given key (30114) and the sequence is not exhausted so move to next item, stock number 30115

and repeat the loop.

The current key (30115) is greater than the given key so the loop terminates and the insertion is made immediately *before* the current item (i.e. before the third record: Caster sugar).

Finally the size of the sequence is increased from 4 to 5.

2 (a) The stock number is the key field.

  (b) (i) Use the key search method shown in Figure 2.2 but with the *stock number* in place of the *time* field and the *number of cases* in place of the *source* field.

     (ii) Use the non-key search of Figure 2.3 with the *description* field in place of the *source* field and the *number of cases* in place of the *time* field.

2.4 Deletion

Before attempting to delete an item from a sequence, it is necessary to know whether the item is definitely there to be deleted. In other words, we must first find the specified item in the sequence and then remove it, or, if the item is not found, report its absence. The search may be a *key search* or a *non-key search*. When applied to the flight sequence in Figure 2.1, the requirement may be, for example, to delete the record for the 17.45 arrival (involving a *key search*), or to delete the *next* arrival from *Glasgow* (which requires a *non-key search*), or to delete the 17.50 arrival (using another *key search*) – which is not possible, because there is no such record in the sequence.

2.5 Other operations on sequences

Retrieval of data from a sequence, the *insertion* of a new item and *deletion* of an existing item are the main operations associated with a sequence. In all of these operations, *searching* a sequence to determine the presence or absence of specified data, or to find where to put new data is of fundamental importance.

Updating

Before an item can be updated by assigning a new value to one or more of its fields, the item must be located by searching the sequence. When the updating involves assignment to the key field of a specified record it may be necessary also to rearrange the items to restore the order of the sequence. In the flight sequence example, if the next flight from *Belfast* is delayed by twenty minutes the updating process can be performed in three stages:

1 Search for the item with *source* equal to *Belfast*.
2 Update the *time* field of the specified item.
3 Restore the order of the sequence.

The rearrangement is easily performed by deletion of the existing item and insertion of a new item containing updated values. However, this is an implementation detail which we shall pursue later.

Interrogation of size

The only remaining operation from those listed at the beginning of Section 2 is *interrogation of the size* of a sequence. The most common use of this operation is the special case: testing a sequence to see if it is empty. Very few operations can be associated with an empty sequence: the '*is_empty*' test is one; *insertion* is another. You may recall that in the previous *Units II.1* and *II.2* we referred briefly to the size of an array, noting that there was no use for an array with no elements. In contrast, when processing a sequence, we must always be aware of the possibility that it is empty.

2.6 Summary of section

This section briefly reviews the definition of the abstract data type *sequence* and operations associated with a sequence: *creation* and *initialization*; *insertion*, *deletion* and *retrieval* of information; *updating* information in a sequence and determining whether a sequence contains any items of data or is empty. It is noted that searching is a fundamental operation associated with a general sequence.

3 Representation of a sequence

In general, sequences are not provided as standard data structures in high-level programming languages. It is, therefore, necessary to implement them, using the 'built-in' data structures which are available in the language. We shall look at two techniques:

(i) The items forming the sequence are placed in memory in the same order as they occur in the *sequence*. This is known as *contiguous representation* and forms the subject of the remainder of this unit.

(ii) The items forming the sequence are *not* stored in the order in which they occur in the sequence. In this case, each item is given an additional field, called a **link**, which is used to indicate the order. This is known as **linked representation** and will be studied in *Unit 3*.

Before going any further, we must stress that an implementation of an abstract data structure, in this case a sequence, may produce a concrete data structure with some additional properties which the sequence itself does not possess. From the point of view of the implementor – probably a systems programmer – this is a fact of which he should take full advantage. In general, however, the user will remain in ignorance of the changes. So far as he is concerned, a sequence has been implemented as just a sequence, with no change in its properties. It is important that you should bear in mind, during your reading of these sections, from which point of view – that of the implementor or that of the user – the topic is currently being considered.

3.1 Contiguous representation

Our first method of implementing a sequence, with its associated operations uses a record with the following fields:

(i) An integer called *size*.

(ii) A one-dimensional table called *item**.

(iii) An integer called *limit*.

The technique is illustrated in Figure 3.1, which represents the same sequence as Figure 2.1. The data items are stored in the table, with the first element of the sequence in *item*[1]. The table element which currently holds the last item in the sequence is indexed by the value held in *size*, which also tells us the total number of items currently in the sequence. The integer *limit* indexes the last element in the table and thus stores the maximum number of items which the sequence can have. The value of *limit* must be carefully chosen, so that the table is large enough to hold the maximum length to which the sequence is likely to grow. As Figure 3.1 shows, only elements *item*[1] to *item*[5] currently hold values.

				time	source
size	5	*item*	1	16.00	Manchester
			2	17.05	Glasgow
limit	100		3	17.30	Belfast
			4	17.45	Dublin
			5	18.00	Bristol
			6		
		100			

Figure 3.1 *A contiguous representation of the sequence shown in Figure 2.1*

SAQ 3.1

What is meant by a contiguous representation of a data structure?

Solution 3.1

The items in a contiguous representation are stored in adjacent locations. This means that, if an element is to be inserted or deleted, then, in general, some existing elements have to be moved. An array is the most typical and useful example of a contiguous data structure.

A wide range of operations can be provided to manipulate this representation of the sequence, some of which will now be explained.

* *item* is a **table** – a one-dimensional array of records. Being an array, *item* provides a contiguous representation.

3.2 Implementation of a general sequence

Some of the operations on a general sequence are quite straight forward. For example, initialization simply requires the size of the sequence to be set to zero, representing an empty sequence, and the value of *limit* to be set to the upper bound of the array or table in which the elements are represented. Other operations, including insertion, retrieval and deletion, are slightly more involved because they can be performed at any point in the sequence, so insertion and deletion generally require some elements to be moved.

We noted in Section 2.2 that retrieving data from a sequence into which a number of items have already been inserted involves *searching*. To facilitate this searching it is convenient to extend the representation of our sequence by including an additional (dummy) element with index zero. You will recall that this technique was used when searching arrays in *Block II*.

				time	source
size	5	item	0		
			1	16.00	Manchester
limit	100		2	17.05	Glasgow
			3	17.30	Belfast
			4	17.45	Dublin
			5	18.00	Bristol
			6		
			100		

Figure 3.2

We said that the search must start with the first item in the sequence and that no other element can be accessed without first accessing its *predecessor* in the sequence. This is consistent with the user's view of a sequence. However, we have also stressed that an implementation of an abstract data structure, in this case a sequence, may produce a concrete data structure with some additional properties which the sequence itself does not possess (e.g. a representation in an array permits access to any indexed element). The implementor can take advantage of the additional properties to simplify the implementation of associated operations. Now a table, being an array of records, provides a contiguous

representation in which the individual items can be accessed in any order by means of an index value which can be calculated. If we know the index to the last item, for example, we can access its predecessor by decrementing the index value and so on, working backwards through the representation of the sequence. In our representation of the flight sequence as a table, the variable *size* is an index to the last item. We shall use this as our starting point and search backwards through the sequence. The advantages of this method will soon become clear.

3.2.1 Retrieval

We start with the retrieval of data from a *non-key field*, given the value in the *corresponding key field*. Suppose that in our flight sequence (see Figure 3.2) we are asked to find the source of the flight due at *17.45*. Clearly, we have to search through the entries in the *time* field for the value *17.45* and, in so doing, we use the fact that the values in the *time* field are ordered. If the sequence is fairly short, then a simple linear search will be best. An appropriate initial process called *linearkeysearch* works as follows:

1 Place the given time in the time field of *item[0]*.
2 Start at the end of the sequence.
3 Search backwards through the sequence for a time *less than* or *equal to* the given item.

We express it more formally in Pascal as shown in Figure 3.3

```
item[0].time := timegiven;
p := size;
while item[p].time > timegiven do
    p := p − 1
```

Figure 3.3

On exit from this process:

either $p = 0$, which indicates that the wanted value is not present

or $p <> 0$, in which case
$item[p].time <= timegiven$ and
$item[p + 1].time > timegiven$.

For example, if we use *linearkeysearch* to find $timegiven = 17.45$, then index p will be set equal to 4 since $item[4].time = 17.45$.

Clearly, if $p <> 0$, we know only that *timegiven may* be present in the table. We then need to test whether

item[p].time = timegiven

Before you read on, compare this process, *linearkeysearch*, with the process design given in Figure 2.2. The simpler structure of *linearkeysearch* is immediately apparent. To achieve this improvement we have:

(i) Ensured that the given key value is always found, even when the sequence is empty, by inserting the required value in *item*[0], which immediately precedes the first item of the sequence.

(ii) Searched backwards from the last item, *item*[size], until the required item is found and without having to check on each iteration to see if the sequence is exhausted. If the search terminates with $p = 0$, then the required data is not present in the actual sequence, for *item*[0] is not in the sequence.

When the sequence in which we want to search is long, it is more efficient to use a binary search, as described in *Block II*.

Exercise 3.1 _____

In what circumstances can the binary search be used to find the location of a specific item in a sequence?

Armed with the familiar searching routines, we can now describe a method for finding where the flight due at a given time originated. The process is shown in the design in Figure 3.4.

```
1   use keysearch to search for the given
                    time in the time field
2   if it is not found
3   then
4       report that there is no such time
5   else
6       pick up the required source from
                    the corresponding source field
7   ifend
```

Figure 3.4

Technically, *keysearch* is the name of a routine which carries out the task of searching *item*: it represents either *linearkeysearch* or *binarykeysearch* or whatever searching routine we choose to use.

Now let us consider the retrieval of information from a key field given the value in a corresponding *non-key* field. Using the

same example, suppose we wish to find the time at which the Glasgow flight is due to arrive. Since the values in a non-key field are *not ordered*, we shall need to search through the complete sequence, possibly, for an item with *Glasgow* in its *source* field. Once again, we separate the search from the retrieval process.

An appropriate technique for the *nonkeysearch* is shown in the design that follows:

```
1   place the given source in item[0].source
2   start at the end of the sequence
3   search backwards through the sequence for a source equal
        to the given source
```

The *nonkeysearch* is very similar to *linearkeysearch*, except that it terminates at *item*[0], indicating that the given value is not present, or before reaching *item*[0], in which case the given value is *definitely* present.

For example, using the *nonkeysearch* routine to look for *Belfast* (Figure 3.1), will finish at *item*[3]; while searching for *Liverpool* will finish at *item*[0], since *Liverpool* is not present.

SAQ 3.2 _____

What value of p would be returned as a result of executing the following operations on the sequence in Figure 3.1?

(i) A *linearkeysearch* to look for *17.30*.

(ii) A *linearkeysearch* to look for *18.30*.

(iii) A *nonkeysearch* to look for *Dublin*.

(iv) A *nonkeysearch* to look for *Edinburgh*.

Solution 3.2

(i) $p = 3$,   (ii) $p = 5$,   (iii) $p = 4$,   (iv) $p = 0$.

So, to construct the complete retrieval process, we have the design shown in Figure 3.5.

```
1   use nonkeysearch to search for the given source
                            in the source field
2   if it is not found
3   then
4       report that there is no such source
5   else
6       pick up the required time from the corresponding time field
7   ifend
```

Figure 3.5

So if we are given some data and asked to find some corresponding data held in a sequence, the method we shall use will depend on whether the given data occurs in a key field or in a non-key field. (You may have realized that the non-key search technique can be applied to a key field but, of course, it is not as efficient.)

SAQ 3.3

(a) How is a sequence searched for either a given key field value or a given non-key field value?

(b) What is the essential difference between a keysearch and a non-key search?

Solution 3.3

(a) All searching of a sequence is normally done by starting with the first item and working through the sequence item by item, until the required item is found (if it exists). However, a contiguous representation of a sequence as a table permits a simpler search procedure starting with the last element and working backwards until the required item is found.

(b) The essential difference between a keysearch and a non-key search is in the way they terminate when the required item is not present; the *key search, taking advantage of the ordering, terminates at the point at which the required item would be located if present* whereas the *non-key search has to examine every item in the sequence* before determining the *absence* of the required item.

Exercise 3.2

The table in Figure 3.6 represents a sequence of records held in alphabetical order, by name:

			code	name
size	6	item 0		
		1	74162	body
limit	100	2	74208	head
		3	74317	left-arm
		4	74412	left-leg
		5	74318	right-arm
		6	74413	right-leg
		7		
		100		

Figure 3.6

Write a module design, based on the outline designs we have supplied earlier, for each of the following operations:

(i) *codefor* (*namegiven, codewanted*), which will assign to *codewanted* the code for the part named *namegiven*;

(ii) *nameof* (*codegiven, namewanted*), which will assign to *namewanted* the name for the part with code *codegiven*.

3.2.2 Insertion

When a new item is inserted in a sequence it must be put in at exactly the right place. In our example of flight arrivals this means inserting each new item so as to maintain the correct chronological order. If, for example (*17.15, Cardiff*) is to be inserted it must go between (*17.05, Glasgow*) and (*17.30, Belfast*). Consequently, in our representation of the sequence as a table, a space has to be created between these two items, which in turn requires that the items for *Belfast, Dublin* and *Bristol* must all be moved. A possible first outline for the required process is shown in Figure 3.7.

```
1   with sequence do
2     if there is no room
3     then
4        write out 'sequence in full'
5     else
6        find where new item should go
7        move other items (if necessary) to make room for it
8        insert new item
9        set size of sequence to size of sequence + 1
10    ifend
```

Figure 3.7

You will see that we have used 'with' in our designs in the same way that it is used in Pascal.

The check on the available space is necessary because the sequence is being represented in an array (of records – a table) which, by definition, is of fixed length, so that there may not be room for another item.

If we insert (*17.15, Cardiff*) the main stages are as shown in Figure 3.9. This insertion process can be implemented as in Figure 3.8. Notice that the movement of items to make room for the new item starts with the last item of the sequence and terminates when the position for the insertion is reached.

There are three points to note:

(i) The searching process sets *p* as the index of the item immediately *before* the point at which the new item is to go in.

(ii) The value *17.15* is left in *item*[0].*time* by the searching process, but is not part of the sequence.

(iii) The value (*17.30, Belfast*) actually exists twice at the stage when the moving has

14

insert1

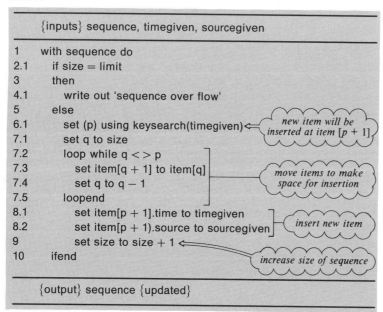

```
{inputs} sequence, timegiven, sourcegiven

1      with sequence do
2.1      if size = limit
3        then
4.1        write out 'sequence over flow'
5        else
6.1        set (p) using keysearch(timegiven)
7.1        set q to size
7.2        loop while q < > p
7.3          set item[q + 1] to item[q]
7.4          set q to q − 1
7.5        loopend
8.1          set item[p + 1].time to timegiven
8.2          set item[p + 1).source to sourcegiven
9            set size to size + 1
10         ifend

{output} sequence {updated}
```

new item will be inserted at item [p + 1]

move items to make space for insertion

insert new item

increase size of sequence

Figure 3.8

		time	source
size 5	*item* 0		
	1	*16.00*	*Manchester*
limit 100	2	*17.05*	*Glasgow*
	3	*17.30*	*Belfast*
	4	*17.45*	*Dublin*
	5	*18.00*	*Bristol*
	6		
	7		
	100		

(a) Find where (*17.15 Cardiff*) should go in

		time	source
size 5	*item* 0	*17.15*	
	1	*16.00*	*Manchester*
limit 100	2	*17.05*	*Glasgow*
	3	*17.30*	*Belfast*
	4	*17.30*	*Belfast*
	5	*17.45*	*Dublin*
	6	*18.00*	*Bristol*
	7		
	100		

(b) Move other items to make room

		time	source
size 6	*item* 0	*17.15*	
	1	*16.00*	*Manchester*
limit 100	2	*17.05*	*Glasgow*
	3	*17.15*	*Cardiff*
	4	*17.30*	*Belfast*
	5	*17.45*	*Dublin*
	6	*18.00*	*Bristol*
	7		
	100		

(c) Insert the new item

Figure 3.9 *Stages in inserting an item, using insert1*

been completed, but one of these instances is no longer a proper element in the sequence, as is indicated by the shading in Figure 3.9(b), and will be overwritten when the new item is inserted in record 3.

The only refinement still required is to convert this module to a Pascal procedure. This requires:

(i) source data and results to be expressed as formal parameters in the procedure heading;

(ii) the *set ... using* statement to be refined as a procedure or function call.

Note, however, that if we use *linearkeysearch* then while we were searching for the correct place, we could, at the same time, have done some moving of the elements. It is, therefore, more efficient to combine the two processes as shown in the design in Figure 3.10.

This gives the following module, which is a linear search but does not make explicit use of *linearkeysearch* as shown in *insert2* in Figure 3.11.

You should note that both designs of the *insert* operation work equally as well if the new item has to go in at the beginning, at the end, or somewhere in between. Moreover, the total amount of computation needed to insert a new item is

```
1    with sequence do
2      if there is no more room
3      then
4        write out 'sequence is full'
5      else
6        start at the end of the sequence
7        move each item, which belongs after the new item, along
                                 the table by one element
8        insert new item
9        set size of sequence to size of sequence + 1
10     ifend
```

Figure 3.10

insert2

{inputs} sequence, timegiven, sourcegiven
1   with sequence do
2.1   if size = limit
3   then
4   write out 'sequence is full'
5   else
6.1   set item[0] . time = timegiven
6.2   set p to size
7.1   loop while item[p] . time > timegiven
7.2   set item[p + 1] to item[p]
7.3   set p to p − 1
7.4   loopend
8.1   set item[p + 1] . time to timegiven
8.2   set item[p + 1] . source to sourcegiven
9.1   set size to size + 1
10   ifend
{output} sequence{updated}

Figure 3.11

proportional to the current length of the sequence, since, on average, approximately half of the sequence will be searched to determine where the new item should go in. Similarly, on average, half the existing items must be moved to create the space for the new item. This requirement to move the items is a major disadvantage in the contiguous method of representing a sequence.

Exercise 3.3

Use an *initialization* routine and *insert2* to perform the following sequence of operations, on the variables *size*, *limit* and *item* of the flight sequence (Figure 3.2), showing the state of the data structure after each process:

Initialize.

Insert the record (*8.15, Dublin*).

Insert the record (*7.35, Glasgow*).

Insert the record (*9.20, Bristol*).

Insert the record (*7.35, Glasgow*).

Exercise 3.4

As you will have discovered from the last exercise, the routine *insert* puts the new item into the sequence even when that item is already present, the new copy being inserted just after any existing copies. If such duplicate values are to be avoided, then the process of searching and moving items up the table must be kept separate.

Produce a top-level design for a module, *insertifabsent*, to insert the record (*timegiven, sourcegiven*) in the table *item*, provided that the record is *not* already present in the table. Your solution should be based on the module *insert1*.

3.2.3 Deletion

Before attempting to delete an item from a sequence, it is necessary to know whether the item is definitely there to be deleted.

When applied to the flight sequence in Figure 3.2, then an appropriate *delete* process is as shown in Figure 3.12.

1   with sequence do
2   search for item to be deleted
3   if it is not present
4   then
5   write out 'no such item present'
6   else
7   move the items (if any) which follow the one to be deleted, one step towards the beginning of the sequence
8   set size of sequence to size of sequence − 1
9   ifend

Figure 3.12

Two more formal versions of this process are given: the former, *timedelete* (Figure 3.13), is to be used when the item to be deleted is defined by the *time* field (the *key* field), and the latter, *sourcedelete* (Figure 3.14), when it is defined by the *source* field (the *non-key* field). The only difference lies in the search process which is used.

timedelete

{input} sequence, timegiven
1   with sequence do
2.1   set(p) using keysearch(timegiven)
3.1   if (p = 0) or (item[p].time < > timegiven)
4   then
5   write out 'no such item present'
6   else
7.1   loop while p < > size
7.2   set item[p] to item[p + 1]
7.3   set p to p + 1
7.4   loopend
8.1   set size to size − 1
9   ifend
{output} sequence {updated}

Figure 3.13

sourcedelete

{input} sequence, sourcegiven
1   with sequence do
2.1   set (p) using nonkeysearch (sourcegiven)
3.1   if p = 0
4   then
5   write out 'no such item present'
6   else
7.1   loop whie p < > size
7.2   set item [p] to item [p + 1]
7.3   set p to p + 1
7.4   loopend
8.1   set size to size − 1
9   ifend
{output} sequence {updated}

Figure 3.14

Exercise 3.5

Given the data structure in Figure 3.15, show the state of the data structure after performing each of the following successive operations:

(i) *source delete* is used to remove *Oslo*.

(ii) *timedelete* is used to remove *2.05*.

(iii) *sourcedelete* is used to remove *Oslo*.

(iv) *sourcedelete* is used to remove *Zurich*.

For operations (ii), (iii) and (iv) state also the value of *p* after the searching process and the number of items moved.

3.3 Summary of section

(i) Two methods which can be used to represent a sequence of items in the main store of a computer are *contiguous representation* and *linked representation*.

(ii) A *contiguous representation* uses a one-dimensional array, or table, the *size* of which is chosen to accommodate the maximum length to which the sequence might grow.

(iii) Operations on the sequence frequently involve *searching*, and the available methods of searching depend on whether the search is to use a *key* field or a *non-key* field. A non-key search can be applied to a key field but is not so efficient.

(iv) When using a contiguous representation, an *insertion* or *deletion* involves *moving*, on average, half of the items in the sequence. This is the main disadvantage of a contiguous representation.

		time	source
size [5] *item* 0			
1		*1.45*	*Paris*
limit [100] 2		*2.05*	*Rome*
3		*2.30*	*Oslo*
4		*3.15*	*Berlin*
5		*3.40*	*Zurich*
6			
100			

Figure 3.15

4 *Stacks*

Now we shall consider a particular kind of sequence on which the following limited range of insertion and deletion operations only is allowed:

(i) A *new* item can be *inserted* only at the *end* of the sequence, i.e. *after* all the existing items.

(ii) The *last* item only in the sequence can be retrieved or deleted.

A sequence to which these restrictions apply is called a **stack** and the end at which the insertions and deletions take place is commonly called the **top** of the stack. A stack is, therefore, a sequence in which the order of the items is determined not by the values of the data items (as in the case of our sequence of flight arrivals), but simply *by the order in which they were inserted.* An item which is removed from a stack is always the one which was most recently added – it is a case of *last in, first out,* which we often refer to as *LIFO.*

Sometimes it helps to understand the mechanism of a stack in terms of an analogy from the switching of railway wagons as shown in Figure 4.1.

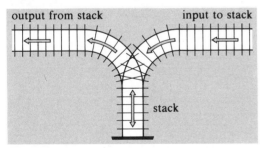

Figure 4.1 *A stack represented as a railway switching network*

An everyday example of a stack is a pile of plates in a cafeteria. Plates are removed from the top of the pile and clean plates are placed on top of the pile.

4.1 Operations on a stack

The operations of insertion, retrieval and deletion are particularly simple when applied to a stack because they take place *only* at the *top* of the stack and no searching is necessary.

Inserting an item on a stack is normally called **pushing** the item on the stack. The combined operation of retrieving an item and then *deleting* it from the stack is called **popping** the item from the stack. Clearly, it is not possible to pop an item from an empty stack, so when using a stack we must always ensure that it is not empty before we attempt to pop an item from it. For this reason, one of the operations normally associated with a stack is an *is_empty* operation to test the state of the stack. One further facility must be available to the programmer who wishes to use a stack; this is the facility to create a stack and prepare it for use. For most practical purposes, a stack is created with a certain capacity, i.e. with a given size, which is the maximum number of items which can be held in the stack at any time. Any attempt to exceed this maximum number of items will result in a condition known as **overflow**. In similar terms, an attempt to pop an empty stack is said to result in **underflow**.

We have introduced several new terms in the context of operations on a stack. Some examples and exercises will help you to understand the mechanism of a stack and to become familiar with the terminology associated with it. First let us specify some Pascal routines which implement the operations on a stack. As a user of these routines you need not concern yourself with how the routines are implemented; you only need to know how to use them.

procedure *push (item : item_type;* **var** *s : stack);*

{This procedure accepts an *item* and inserts (or pushes) it on a stack *s*. Notice that *s* is a **var** parameter because the state of the stack is changed by this operation; on exit from the procedure the stack will contain the additional item. The type *item_type* will need to be defined, we shall return to this later but for the present let us assume that *item_type* can be any one of *integer*, or *character*, or *real*, or *string*, or anything else we require, and that *stack* is defined to hold items of type *item_type*. If the stack *s* is already full on entry to this procedure, then overflow will occur; this is a 'fatal error' condition, and there is no option but to abort the program.}

procedure *pop* (**var** *s*: *stack;*
      var *item*: *item_type*);

{The *pop* procedure retrieves and deletes the top item from the stack. Hence both *item* and *s* are **var** parameters. If the stack *s* is empty when this procedure is entered, underflow will occur; this is another 'fatal error'.}

function *is_empty* (*s*: *stack*) : *Boolean;*

{The *is_empty* function returns *true* if the stack *s* contains no elements and *false* otherwise.}

procedure *initialize* (**var** *s*: *stack*);

{The *initialize* procedure prepares a stack for use. Just as a variable must be assigned a value before it can be used, so also a stack must be set initially to empty.}

Assume that type *item_type* is defined as

type *item_type* = *string;*

and that type stack is so defined that the declaration

var *s*: *stack;*

creates a stack *s* capable of holding items of type *string*. Then consider the program in Figure 4.2 in which we have numbered some of the statements so that we may refer to them.

Let us trace the execution of these statements. Figure 4.3 shows the state of the stack immediately after execution of each of the statements numbered (1), (2), (3) and (4).

contains implementation of stack and associated operations

```
program stack_of_names;
uses  stackunit;
var s: stack;        {create a stack s}
     item: string;
begin
   initialize (s);                          (1)
   push('Mary', s);                         (2)
   push('Tom', s);                          (3)
   pop(s, item);                            (4)
   push('Jane', s);                         (5)
   push('Paul', s);                         (6)
   pop(s, item);                            (7)
   pop(s, item);                            (8)
   pop(s, item);                            (9)
   if is_empty(s)                          (10)
   then
       push('Joe', s)                      (11)
   else
       pop(s, item);                       (12)
   {do nothing}                            (13)
end.
```

Figure 4.2

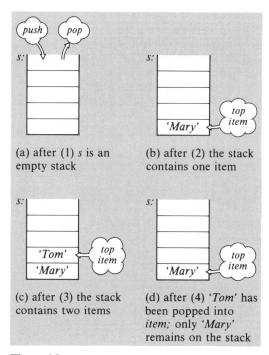

Figure 4.3

SAQ 4.1 _____

(i) Show the state of the stack *s* immediately after execution of the statement in step (7); what is the value assigned to *item* at this point?

(ii) What is the value of *item* immediately after step (9)?

(iii) What is the result of the condition *is_empty*(*s*) in step (10)?

(iv) Show the state of the stack at step (13).

Solution 4.1

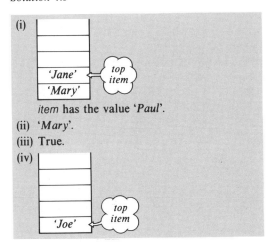

Figure 4.4

4.2 Implementation of a stack

For a stack all operations take place at *one* end called the *top* of the stack. The implementation of the insertion and deletion operations is, therefore, very straightforward. Assuming that the stack is to be used for items of base type *string*, it can be represented as a record with the following three fields:

(i) a one-dimensional array of strings called *item*, with, say, index range 1 to 20;
(ii) an integer variable called *top*;
(iii) an integer variable called *limit*.

Initialization of the stack, which must be done first, can then be implemented as shown in Figure 4.5:

initialize

{input} stack
set stack.top to 0 set stack.limit to 20
{output} stack

Figure 4.5

This simply says that the stack initially contains no items and sets the value of limit equal to the upper bound of the array *item*.

The operation of *pushing* an item on to the stack (i.e. insertion) is shown in Figure 4.6.

Since the insertion takes place at the end of the sequence (the top of the stack), there is

push

{input} datagiven, stack
1 with stack do 2   if top = limit 3   then 4   write out 'stack overflow' 5   else 6   set top to top + 1 7   set item[top] to datagiven 8   ifend
{output} stack

Figure 4.6

no necessity to move any items currently in the sequence.

Popping an item from a stack (i.e. retrieving the top item from the stack while deleting it) can be implemented as shown in Figure 4.7.

pop

{input} stack
1 with stack do 2   if top = 0 3   then 4   write out 'stack underflow' 5   else 6   set datawanted to item[top] 7   set top to top − 1 8   ifend
{output} datawanted, stack

Figure 4.7

You will notice that the procedure *pop* is equivalent to retrieval immediately followed by deletion.

The operation of testing a stack to see if it is empty is particularly simple as you can see from Figure 4.8.

is_empty

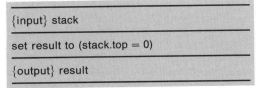

{input} stack
set result to (stack.top = 0)
{output} result

Figure 4.8

In other words, if *stack.top* is zero, *is_empty* is true, otherwise *is_empty* is *false*.

Assuming that each element of a stack can hold a name, draw a sequence of diagrams to illustrate the state of the stack and of the variable *datawanted*, after carrying out each of the following successive operations:

(i) *initializestack* (with limit 20).

(ii) Push the value '*Bill*'.

(iii) Push the value '*Mary*'.

(iv) Pop into *datawanted*.

(v) Push the value '*John*'.

(vi) Push the value '*Jim*'.

4.3 Practical exercise

Requirements

Now we look at a problem which can be solved using a stack. Suppose we have a Pascal expression which includes several sets of nested parentheses and square brackets. For example, consider the character string

x + (y[a + b] − c)/(e + f)

We want to ensure that the parentheses and brackets are nested correctly. (This is one of many checks performed by a Pascal compiler when compiling your programs.)

Expressions such as

((A + B)

A + B[

A + B[C − D)

and

(A + B)) − C(D]

are clearly invalid.

Design

Let us see why a solution to this problem calls for the use of a stack. It is convenient to think of an expression as a string of symbols (i.e. characters); the left parenthesis, (, and left square bracket, [, are substring *openers* and) and] are the matching substring *closers*.

Assume that the expression is scanned from beginning to end. Then, on reaching the end, no substring must remain open. This implies that every *opener* that has been encountered has been matched by a *closer* of the appropriate type.

At each point in the expression where a *closer* is encountered, that *closer* must be matched by the last *opener* that has not

been previously matched. In other words, the last substring to be opened must be the first to be closed.

This last condition is precisely simulated by the use of a stack where the last item to be *pushed* is the first to be *popped*. When an *opener* is encountered it is *pushed* onto the stack. Each item on the stack represents a substring that has been opened but has not yet been closed. When a *closer* is encountered:

- If the stack is empty, there is no matching opener and the expression is invalid.
- Else, if the top item on the stack does not match the current closer, then the expression is invalid.
- Else, if the top item matches the current closer, then the expression as matched so far is valid.

For correct termination, the stack *must be empty* when the string is exhausted.

A process to perform the required check works as shown in the design in Figure 4.9. The stack used in this design holds items of type character.

```
1    initialize a stack
2    set valid to true
3    start at the beginning of the string
4    loop while valid is true and characters remain to be processed
5        if current character is in ['(', ')', '[', ']']
6        then
7            select case depending on current character
8                '(', '[': push current character on stack
9                ')', ']': if stack is empty
10                        then
11                            set valid to false
12                        else
13                            pop stack item into last_opener
14                            if last_opener matches current character
15                            then do nothing
16                            else set valid to false
17                            ifend
18                        ifend
19            selectend
20        else
21            do nothing
22        ifend
23        move to next character of string
24    loopend
25    if stack is not empty
26    then
27        set valid to false
28    ifend
```

Figure 4.9 *A process to check the bracket structure of an expression*

On completion of this process, *valid is true if and only if* the parenthesis and bracket structure of the expression is valid.

Implementation

The Course Team has implemented a stack capable of holding up to twenty items of type *char*, together with the operations *initialize*, *push*, *pop* and *is_empty* as described above.

Your task is to refine the program design given in Figure 4.9 using the template **PCHECK**, and hence to implement and test a Pascal program which, using the stack operations provided, inputs an expression represented as a character string, validates its parenthesis and bracket structure and reports the results.

Test your program on each of the following expressions:

(i) $(a + [b − c]) * (c − d)$

(ii) $((a + b)$

(iii) $a + b [c − d)$

(iv) $x + (y[a + b] − c)/(e + f)$

The programs that you will need to copy on to your user disk are:

B4:UCHECK.CODE
B4:PCHECK.TEXT

If you wish to check the solution for this exercise you will also need to copy **B4:ACHECK.TEXT**.

4.4 Summary of section

If *insertions* and *deletions must be done at one end of a sequence* that sequence is known as a *stack*. The *order of data items in a stack* is determined by the *order in which they were inserted*. The end where the operations take place is called the *top* of the stack. No searching is necessary to locate the top and no movement of other items is involved when the top item is *popped* from the stack or a new item *pushed* onto the stack. Any attempt to pop an empty stack will result in *underflow*. *Overflow* arises when the capacity of a stack is exceeded. Both underflow and overflow are error conditions.

A practical exercise involving the use of a stack gives a user's view of the abstract data type stack.

5 *Queues*

5.1 Introduction

Now we shall consider the implementation of a sequence on which the following limited range of insertion and deletion operations only is allowed:

(i) A new item can be inserted at the end of the sequence *only*, i.e. *after* all the existing items.

(ii) *Only* the first item in the sequence can be deleted or retrieved.

Such a sequence is called a **queue**. The end, at which all insertions take place, is the **rear** of the queue, while deletions and retrievals take place at the **front** of the queue. Thus, a queue is similar to a stack in being a sequence in which the order of the data items is determined not by their values, but simply by the order in which they were inserted. For such a queue, the rule is *first-in, first-out*, which is often referred to as *FIFO*.

Exercise 5.1 _____

When is it possible to retrieve immediately an item which has just been inserted in a queue?

SAQ 5.1 _____

For each of the following, state whether the organization of the objects concerned conforms to our definition of a queue, a stack, or neither. Give reasons for your answers.

(i) Persons waiting at a bus stop.

(ii) The contents of a tube of smarties.

(iii) Patients in the waiting room at a dental surgery.

(iv) The carriages of a train passing through a railway tunnel.

(v) A pile of hand-held wire baskets provided for the use of customers in a supermarket.

(vi) Cars entering and leaving a car park.

Solution 5.1

(i) The normal convention is that the person who has been waiting the longest boards the bus first, so this is a FIFO queue.

(ii) There is no particular order in which smarties are removed from their tube, so this is neither a queue nor a stack.

(iii) Patients may arrive at any time before their appointment so this is not necessarily a FIFO queue; it is definitely not a stack.

(iv) The first carriage to enter the tunnel is the first to emerge at the other end so this is a FIFO queue.

(v) The baskets are normally taken from the top of the pile, so this is a LIFO stack.

(vi) The time for which any car is parked is generally independent of the time of arrival at the car park so this is neither a queue nor a stack.

5.2 Operations on a queue

The fundamental operations on a queue are very similar to those for a stack; only the order in which items are retrieved and deleted is different. Since insertion, retrieval and deletion are performed at the end of the queue, no searching is necessary and no items have to be moved to make space for an insertion or close a gap following a deletion. Overflow and underflow conditions can arise in the same way as for a stack.

You will recall that for a stack, insertion and deletion are conventionally referred to as *push* and *pop* operations. There is no similar convention for a queue although some texts refer to *queue* and *unqueue* operations. We shall use the terms *insert* and *remove*.

Assume that a data type *queue* has been defined to hold items of some type *item_type* and that operations on a queue are implemented by the following Pascal routines:

```
procedure initialize (var q: queue);
{This procedure prepares a queue for use, setting the number
                        of items in the queue to zero}

procedure insert (var q: queue; item: item_type);
{If the queue is already full, overflow is reported otherwise the given
item is added to the specified queue. Overflow is a 'fatal error'}

procedure remove (var q: queue; var item: item_type);
{If the specified queue is not empty, the item at the front of the queue
is retrieved, assigned to item and deleted from the queue. An attempt
to remove an item from an empty queue results in underflow}

function empty (q: queue): Boolean;
{If the specified queue contains no elements, then
empty returns true, otherwise false is returned}
```

Now assume that type *item_type* is defined as

```
type item_type = string;
```

and that type *queue* is so defined that the declaration

```
var q: queue;
```

creates a queue q capable of holding items of type *string*.

Let us now trace the execution of the statements in Figure 5.1. The effect of statement (1) is to create an empty queue. The state of the queue and the variable *item* after execution of each of the statements numbered (2) to (5) is shown in Figure 5.2.

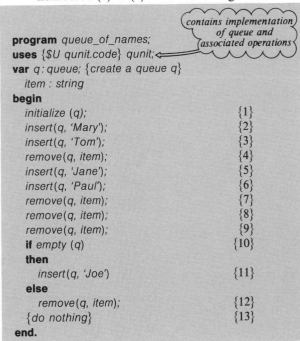

```
program queue_of_names;                        contains implementation
uses {$U qunit.code} qunit;                     of queue and
var q: queue; {create a queue q}               associated operations
 item : string
begin
  initialize (q);                                {1}
  insert(q, 'Mary');                             {2}
  insert(q, 'Tom');                              {3}
  remove(q, item);                               {4}
  insert(q, 'Jane');                             {5}
  insert(q, 'Paul');                             {6}
  remove(q, item);                               {7}
  remove(q, item);                               {8}
  remove(q, item);                               {9}
  if empty (q)                                  {10}
  then
    insert(q, 'Joe')                            {11}
  else
    remove(q, item);                            {12}
  {do nothing}                                  {13}
end.
```

Figure 5.1

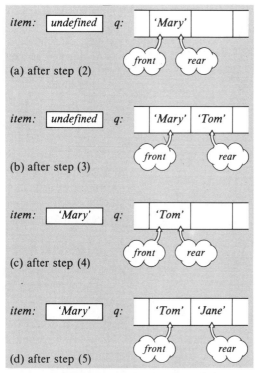

Figure 5.2 *The state of the queue q and the variable item after steps (2) to (5) of the program in Figure 5.1*

SAQ 5.2

(i) Show the state of the queue q and give the value of *item* immediately *after* execution of the statement numbered (7).

(ii) What is the value of *item* immediately *after* statement (9)?

(iii) Show the state of the queue and the value of *item* at statement (13).

Solution 5.2

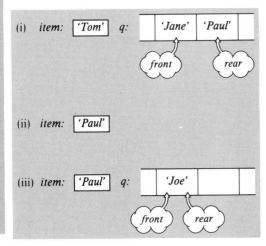

Figure 5.3

5.3 Implementation of a queue

One way in which a queue can be represented using contiguous allocation of storage is as a record containing the following fields:

(i) A one-dimensional array of items (or a table) called *item* with, say, index of 1..100 (hence the maximum number of items in the queue is 100).

(ii) An integer value called *limit*, being the maximum capacity of the queue (100 in this case).

(iii) Two integer variables called *front* and *rear*, being indexes to the first and last items, respectively, in the queue.

(iv) An integer variable called *size*, being the number of elements currently contained in the queue.

Figure 5.4(a) illustrates a queue containing three items *A*, *B* and *C* and having a maximum capacity of five items. *A* is at the front of the queue, *C* is at the rear. Figure 5.4(b) shows the same queue after one item has been removed. Since only the item at the front of the queue can be removed, *A* is

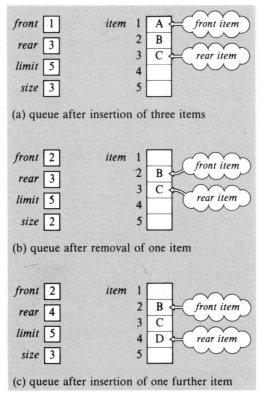

(a) queue after insertion of three items

(b) queue after removal of one item

(c) queue after insertion of one further item

Figure 5.4 *Representation of a queue*

removed and *B* is now at the front. Figure 5.4(c) shows the queue after the insertion of a further item, *D*. *D* is now the rear item.

The queue in Figure 5.4 can be obtained by following the sequence of operations:

```
initialize (q); {initialize a queue}
insert (q, A); {insert an item, A, in the queue, q}
insert (q, B);
insert (q, C);
remove (q, x); {remove front item from q and
                              assign it to x}
insert (q, D)
```

Let us examine further what might happen under this representation. Figure 5.5 shows the state of the queue after performing the further operations

remove(q, y);
insert(q, E)

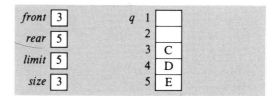

Figure 5.5

The queue now contains only three items: *C*, *D* and *E*; it has a capacity of five items, so it should be possible to insert two further items before the queue becomes full. However, to insert a further item, *F*, is not quite so straightforward. Either we must move the existing items *C*, *D* and *E* up the array to make room for the additional item at the rear, or we must devise a method for making use of those locations which are available. The first possibility might be suitable for a queue with small capacity but for a long queue many items must be moved each time the upper bound of the array is reached and this is considered to be impractical. Another solution is to treat the array that holds the queue as a *circle* (see Figure 5.6), in which the *first element* of the array *immediately follows* (in a clockwise sense) the *last element*. This implies that even if the last element, *q[limit]*, is occupied, a new item can be inserted 'behind' it in the first element, *q[1]*, of the array.

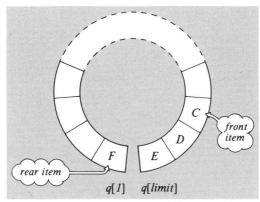

Figure 5.6 *Representation of a queue as an array viewed as a circle*

5.4 Queues in Pascal

A queue of strings, say, can be declared and initialized as shown in Figure 5.7

```
const maxqueue = 100; {or some other predetermined limit}
type queue = record
                 item: array [1..maxqueue] of string;
                 front, rear: 1..maxqueue;
                 size: 0..maxqueue
             end;
var q1, w2, q3: queue;
procedure initialize(var q: queue);
begin
    q.front:= 1;
    q.rear:= maxqueue;
    q.size:= 0
end;
      .
      .
      .
begin
    initialize(q1);
    initialize(q2);
```

Figure 5.7

We have chosen to initialize *front* to the *lower* bound and *rear* to the *upper* bound of the index to the array because, in our circular representation, the last element of the array immediately precedes the first, so when an item is inserted in the queue, *rear* is advanced one position by the statement:

```
if rear = maxqueue
then rear:= 1
else rear:= rear + 1
```

When the first item is inserted, *rear* is advanced from *maxqueue* to 1 and the first item is placed in *q[1]* (Figure 5.8).

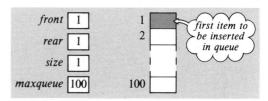

Figure 5.8 *Queue after first insertion of an item*

Similarly, when an item is removed from the queue, *front* is advanced by one position:

```
if front = maxqueue
then front:= 1
else front:= front + 1
```

Note that the statements for advancing *front* and *rear* could be expressed more concisely as

```
front:= front mod maxqueue + 1
```

and

```
rear:= rear mod maxqueue + 1
```

where the integer operator **mod** performs integer division and yields the remainder as its result. Thus, for *maxqueue = 100* and *rear = 100*, *rear* **mod** *maxqueue* yields the value *0*; the addition of *1* then advances *rear* to *1* which is precisely what is required. Similarly, for *rear = 4*, say, and *maxqueue = 100*, *rear* **mod** *maxqueue* yields the value *4* and *rear* **mod** *maxqueue + 1* advances *rear* from *4* to *5*.

The *empty* function may be coded as shown in Figure 5.9

```
function empty (q: queue): Boolean;
begin
    if q.size = 0
    then empty:= true
    else empty:= false
end {function empty};
```

Figure 5.9

The *if* statement within the function *empty* can be expressed more concisely as

```
empty:= (q.size = 0)
```

where the relational expression of the right-hand side delivers a Boolean result, *true* or *false*, which is then assigned to *empty*. However, the purpose of this more concise form is less clear than that of the full expression as an *if*-construct and we shall normally adopt the more readable form.

The operation *remove(q, x)* can be coded as shown in Figure 5.10.

```
procedure remove(var q: queue, var x: string);
{procedure to remove the front item from
                                    a queue}
begin
  if empty(q)
  then writeln('queue underflow')
  else
    with q do
      begin
        {retrieve front item}
        x:= item[front];
        {advance front to new front item};
        if front = maxqueue
        then front:= 1
        else front:= front + 1;
        size:= size − 1
      end
end;  {procedure remove}
```

Figure 5.10

The *insert* procedure must take care of *overflow*; it is written as shown in Figure 5.11.

```
procedure insert(var q: queue; x: string);
begin
  with q do
    if size = maxqueue
    then writeln('queue overflow')
    else
      begin
        {advance the rear pointer}
        if rear = maxqueue
        then rear:= 1
        else rear:= rear + 1;
        {insert the item}
        size:= size + 1;
        item [rear]:= x
      end
end;  {procedure insert}
```

Figure 5.11

Exercise 5.2

Assume the declarations and definitions of a queue and the associated operations given in the text but for items of type integer with $maxqueue = 4$. Show, in the form of diagrams similar to those of Figure 5.4 and 5.8 the state of a queue, q, after each of the four starred operations in the following sequence.

initialize (q);   {*(i)}
insert (q, 17);
insert (q, 12);
insert (q, 24); {*(ii)}
remove (q, x); {*(iii)}
insert (q, 6);
remove (q, x);
insert (q, 23); {*(iv)}

Exercise 5.3

The definitions and declarations of a queue as described in the text assume that queue items are of type *string*. What changes are necessary to the representation of a queue as a **record** in Pascal and to the associated routines *initialize*, *empty*, *remove* and *insert* to implement a queue of items of some user defined type called *item_type*?

Exercise 5.4

In the function *empty* as specified in the text, the formal parameter q is specified as a *non*-**var** parameter, whereas in the routines *initialize*, *remove* and *insert*, q is specified as a **var** parameter. Explain why this is necessary.

5.5 Queues in simulation

One of the most useful applications of queues is in *simulation*. A *simulation program* is one that attempts to model a real-world situation in order to learn something about it. Each object and action in the real situation has a representation in the program. If the simulation program successfully mirrors the real world, then the result of the program should mirror the result of the actions being simulated. Thus, it is possible to understand what occurs in the real-world situation without actually observing its occurrence.

Let us look at an example. Suppose a small petrol filling station has two pumps which are usually busy and that the number of cars queuing is such that some potential customers decide not to wait but drive on to the next available filling station. The owner of the filling station might wish to assess the cost effectiveness of installing additional pumps. A computer model of the filling station could provide estimates of queue lengths and average queuing times for different numbers of pumps and for a variety of assumed rates of arrival of customers. The advantage of being able to predict the result of installing additional service points is readily apparent.

This example is typical of many of its kind. Another one, involving a single queue and one or more servers is a bank in which customers arrive for service and, if necessary, form an orderly first-in, first-out queue until there is a cashier free to serve them. The following practical activity models such a system.

5.4.1 *Practical exercise*

The purpose of this practical exercise is:

(i)   To give a realistic practical application of a queue.

(ii) To demonstrate an important modelling technique by attempting to simulate a real-world situation.

(iii) To give you practical experience of taking an existing piece of software and modifying it in order to satisfy an enhanced specification.

The problem

A small bank has only one cashier on duty at the till. The first customer is served immediately on arrival. If subsequent customers arrive while the cashier is busy serving an earlier arrival, they form an orderly *FIFO* queue. As soon as the cashier is finished serving one customer, he starts serving the next customer in the queue (if any), and customers are served in the order in which they arrived, that is, the queue is a *FIFO* queue.

Requirements

A program is required to simulate the operation of the bank for a specified period of time. The data for this program is:

a, the average time (in minutes) between arrivals of customers;

s, the average time (in minutes) required to serve a customer;

and

total_time, the duration of the simulation, representing the time for which the bank is open.

The duration is specified as a number of minutes; customers arrive until this number of minutes after the opening time.

At the end of the simulation the program is to provide the following outputs;

(i)   The total number of customers who arrive at the bank in the simulated time.

(ii) The proportion of customers who arrive when the cashier is not busy and are served immediately.

(iii) The maximum length of the queue.

(iv) The maximum queuing time for any customer.

(v)   The average queuing time for all customers (including those who are served immediately on arrival).

Design

A high-level design for a very rudimentary simulation program is given in Figure 5.12. This basic design is for a program to do no more than generate customer arrivals, insert arrival times in a queue, determine service times and, at the end of each service, either remove data from the queue (if any) and commence the next service, or deal with the next arrival. The queued items in this program are customer arrival times.

Program design

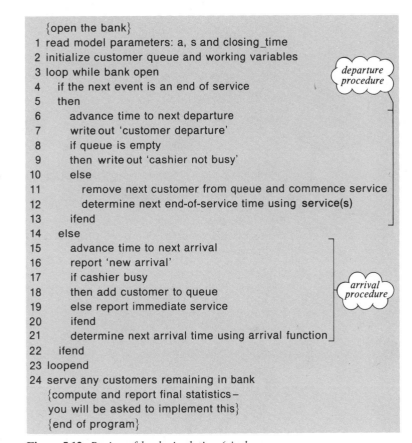

```
{open the bank}
 1 read model parameters: a, s and closing_time
 2 initialize customer queue and working variables
 3 loop while bank open
 4    if the next event is an end of service
 5    then
 6       advance time to next departure
 7       write out 'customer departure'
 8       if queue is empty
 9       then write out 'cashier not busy'
10       else
11          remove next customer from queue and commence service
12          determine next end-of-service time using service(s)
13       ifend
14    else
15       advance time to next arrival
16       report 'new arrival'
17       if cashier busy
18       then add customer to queue
19       else report immediate service
20       ifend
21       determine next arrival time using arrival function
22    ifend
23 loopend
24 serve any customers remaining in bank
   {compute and report final statistics –
   you will be asked to implement this}
   {end of program}
```

departure procedure

arrival procedure

Figure 5.12 *Design of bank simulation (single server, single queue)*

Note that:

(i)   The events which increase the length of the queue are the arrivals of customers while the cashier is busy.

(ii) The events which decrease the length of the queue are the moments when the cashier finishes serving a customer who then departs.

(iii) The only other event is the closing time of the bank.

(iv) In this model time is advanced from one event to the next, i.e. to the next arrival or the next end of service, whichever is the sooner. This continues until closing time, after which any customers in the bank are served but no new arrivals are allowed in.

Using the computer

Your first task is to study the existing bank simulation program which you must understand before you can begin to enhance it. Details of the main procedures are given in the text but you may wish to refer to a continuous listing of the full program in order to see its overall structure. The text of the program is available in **B4:PBANK.TEXT**. In order to do this practical work you will need to copy the following files on to your user disk:

B4:UQUEUE.CODE
B4:USIMM.CODE
B4:PBANK.TEXT

The program uses two precompiled units. The first, *uqueue*, contains the definition of the datatype *queue* together with its associated procedures to *initialize*, *insert* and *remove* items and two functions to test for the special cases of empty queue and full queue.

The second unit, *usimm*, provides two routines which produce sample data values from predefined statistical distributions:

function *arrival* (a : real) : real;

which given the average time, a, between arrivals generates the time (in minutes) between successive customer arrivals; and

function *service* (s : real) : real;

which, given the average time, s, to serve a customer, generates service times for customers.

The *arrival* function makes use of a standard sampling technique, using random numbers, to obtain sample values from a given distribution of intervals between arrivals. The *service* function uses the same technique to obtain samples from a given distribution of service times. The element of randomness models the variations which occur in real life.

Following the well established principle of information hiding, that the user should be told only what he needs to know and not be distracted by what he doesn't need to

know, we are giving no further information about these two routines. You have a specification which includes all the information necessary for their use. You do not need to know how they are implemented.

Now we are ready to consider the bank simulation program from the top-level down, starting with the main program (see Figure 5.13) body which will appear at the end of the complete listing.

```
begin {bank simulation}
  enter_parameters;
  initialize;
  loop_while_bank_open;
  closing;
  writeln('End of simulation');
  writeln;
  print statistics;
  writeln('End of program')
end {bank simulation}
```

Figure 5.13 *Main body of bank simulation program*

The first procedure, *enter_parameters*, prompts the user to input the data for the simulation, i.e. the average time between arrivals, the average service time and the time for which the bank is open. (Such values could be found by observation at the bank.) Next, *initialize* initializes the queue and all the working variables. At the heart of the program is the procedure *loop_while_bank_open* which deals with successive events – customer arrivals, customer service and departures from the bank. This is done by calling two further procedures: *next_arrival* and *next_departure*. We shall return to *loop_while_bank_open* to consider it in more detail.

After closing time no further customers are allowed into the bank. However, it is possible that some customers who arrive before closing time will still be waiting for service when the bank closes. The procedure *closing* deals with any customers remaining in the bank at closing time.

Finally, at the end of the program, any statistics collected during the simulation are output. The existing program produces no statistics. Your task is to enhance it in order to collect and output certain statistics for the operation of the bank.

Now consider the *loop_while_bank_open* statement in the main simulation. This loop (see Figure 5.14) is repeated for as long as customers arrive before closing time. At any time while the bank is open, if the cashier is busy serving a customer and the service of that customer ends before the next customer arrives at the bank, then the next event will be a customer leaving the bank. This event is simulated by the *then* part of the *if* statement (Figure 5.14).

If the cashier is not busy, then there are no customers in the bank and the next event will be a customer arrival. Otherwise, if the cashier is busy and another customer arrives before the end of the current service, then again the next event will be a customer arrival. This event is simulated by the *else* part of the *if* statement. These two kinds of event are dealt with by the procedures *next_departure* and *next_arrival* respectively. You should study these two procedures carefully. They each begin by advancing simulated time to the time of the next event, so time is advanced in discrete steps from one event to the next.

First let us look at *next_departure* (see Figure 5.15).The next event is a customer departure at the end of the current service at time *next_dep* so the current (stimulated) *time* is advanced to *next_dep*. Then, if the queue is empty, no customers are waiting and the cashier becomes idle. Otherwise, if there is a waiting customer, the next customer is removed from the queue and is served. The service time for that customer is obtained by calling *service*, this is added to the current time to determine the time at which this new service will end. Remember that each waiting customer is represented in the queue as a 'customer arrival time'. The current time minus this 'queued' time-of-arrival would tell us how long the customer has been waiting, but as it stands the program makes no use of the time-of-arrival retrieved from the queue.

Now let us look at the procedure *next_arrival* shown in Figure 5.16. Like *next_departure*, this procedure starts by advancing the current (simulated) time to the time of the next event – the next arrival in this case. If the cashier is already busy (serving another customer) then the new arrival must wait in a queue to be served on a first come, first served basis. What is inserted in the queue is this customer's

```
procedure loop_while_bank_open;
begin
  {loop while the next arrival time is earlier than
    the closing time of the bank}
  while next_arr < closing_time do
    begin
      if busy and (next_dep < = next_arr)
      then {next event is a departure}
        next_departure
      else {next event is an arrival}
        next_arrival
    end {loop};
    {no more arrivals before closing time}
  while busy and (next_dep < closing_time) do
    next_departure
end; {loop_while_bank_open}
```

Figure 5.14

```
procedure next_departure;
{deals with customer departure and starts next service}
var
  time_of_arrival: real; {retrieved from queue (if any)}
begin
  {advance current time to next event – the end of current service}
  time: = next_dep;
  write_if_tracing('Departure at time:', time);
  {customer departs, serve next customer (if any)}
  if emptyq(q) {empty queue}
  then {no customer waiting}
    begin {cashier not busy}
      busy: = false;
      write_if_tracing('Empty queue–cashier not busy:', time)
    end
  else {customer waiting in queue}
    begin
      {start serving next customer from the queue}
      removeq(q, time_of_arrival);
      write_if_tracing('Start  next service at time:', time);
      next_dep: = time + service(s)
    end
end; {next departure}
```

Figure 5.15 *Procedure to deal with a customer departure*

arrival time, that is the new current time. If the cashier is not busy, then of course there is no queue and the newly arrived customer can be served immediately. In this case the time at which this service will end is obtained by adding the service time (given by *service*) to the current time. Finally, before returning from *next_arrival*, the time of the next customer arrival is determined as the sum of the current time and the

```
procedure next_arrival;
{deals with the next customer arrival}
begin
    {advance current time to time of next event – an arrival}
    time: = next_arr;
    write_if_tracing('Arrival at time:', time);
    if busy
    then {queue}
        begin
            insertq(time, q)
        end
    else {serve immediately}
        begin
            write_if_tracing('Immediate service:', time);
            busy: = true;
            next_dep: = time + service(s)
        end;
    next_arr: = time + arrival(a)
end; {next arrival}
```

Figure 5.16 *Procedure to deal with a customer arrival*

interval before the next arrival (given by the function *arrival*).

The events are customer arrivals and departures, and appropriate action is taken by the procedures *next_arrival* and *next_departure*, this process of advancing time from event to event, continues until closing time; at closing time the work of the procedure *loop_while_bank_open* is complete and the next procedure, *closing*, is called to deal with any customers remaining in the bank (see Figure 5.17). All this procedure has to do is deal with successive customer service and departures until no more customers remain to be served, at which time the cashier is no longer busy.

```
procedure closing;
begin
    {close the bank and deal with any customers still in the queue}
    write_if_tracing('Bank closing at:', closing_time);
    while busy do
        next_departure
end; {closing}
```

Figure 5.17 *Procedure for serving customers after closing time*

So that you can observe the simulated activities while the program is running, we have included tracing statements to report each event. You should execute the program and study the output obtained. We suggest the following input data for this task:

Average time between arrivals : 5 (min)
Average service time   : 4 (min)
Duration   : 30 (min)

When you are satisfied that you thoroughly understand the existing simulation program you should then enhance it to obtain the required statistics (as specified above and repeated below). We strongly advise you to design, implement and test only one enhancement at a time. When you have implemented as many of the specified requirements as you have time for, turn off the trace output (by giving a negative response to the relevant prompt), leaving only the output of the final statistics, and run your enhanced program for a simulated time of 300 minutes.

Typical output from a fully developed simulation program is shown in Figure 5.18. You should obtain similar results for the given input data values.

Execute what file? ABANK

Enter average time between arrivals : 5
Enter average service time : 4
Enter duration : 300

Do you want tracing? answer Y or N > N

End of simulation

Number of arrivals = 57
    36.94 per cent are served immediately
Cashier busy 65.19 per cent of the time
Maximum queue length = 5
Maximum queuing time = 15.64
Average queuing time = 3.60

End of program

Figure 5.18

It is not expected that you will implement all of the enhancements. **Do not spend more than one evening on this practical activity.**

Required enhancements
Produce the following statistics:

1 The total number of customer arrivals in the simulated time.

2 The proportion of customers who arrive when the cashier is not busy and are served immediately

i.e. $\dfrac{\text{number served immediately}}{\text{total number of arrivals}} * 100$ (per cent).

3 The maximum length of the queue.

4 The maximum time that any customer spends in the queue (from arrival time to start of service).

5 The average queuing time taken over all customers (including those who are served immediately on arrival).

While you still have your enhanced program, check your current TMA to see if there is a question on this practical activity and, if so, whether any further statistics are required.

Finally, before you leave this simulation, we should like you to think about the results you obtained. How realistic are they? Are they roughly what you might have expected from what you know of the operation of a bank for a typical day? Is this a typical day or should the model be run for several days to get a better feeling for the situation? If you are to have any confidence in the results of a simulation you must be convinced that the results are a true reflection of the process being modelled. The simulation should be run more than once. However, for our model this would not be helpful for you would get identical results from each run. The reason is that our random number generator is not truly random; it generates the same sequence of (almost random) numbers each time it is run. So we get the same sequence of arrival times and service times, unless, of course, we vary the parameters passed to *arrival* and *service*. This is useful at the testing stages when we need to be able to reproduce the same results in order to detect and correct any errors, but for normal running of the model some variability should be introduced. After all, no two days in the bank would be identical in all respects. One way of introducing some variability is to run the model with minor changes in the pattern of arrival times and service times. For example you might use a range of values from 4.95 to 5.05 instead of 5.0 minutes for the average time between arrivals. We don't want you to spend more time on this. It is sufficient that you appreciate that the results from a single simulation run are not sufficient to give a reliable indication of how a process operates in practice.

5.6 Priority queues

We conclude this unit with a brief reference to another kind of queue. You may have the impression that all queues have a *FIFO* organization. This is not so. A priority queue is one example of a queue where the order in which items are retrieved is not generally the order of insertion.

A **priority queue** is an ordered sequence of zero or more items in which the first item only can be deleted or retrieved. The order of the items in the queue is determined by their relative priorities and the insertion operation preserves the ordering.

Examples

One example of a priority queue is a queue of programs waiting to be executed by a computer. Programs already in the queue may be overtaken by later arrivals having higher priority.

Another example of a priority queue is a waiting list for hospital beds. Here again a patient whose condition does not require immediate treatment will be overtaken in the queue by other patients requiring more urgent treatment. In an emergency a patient may go straight to the front of the queue and be admitted immediately.

A priority queue could be implemented in the same way as a simple *FIFO* queue. The routines *initialize*, *empty* and *remove* are exactly the same. Only the *insert* procedure is different. New arrivals are so inserted as to preserve the ordering of the sequence. With our representation of a *FIFO* queue in an array, organized as an implicit circle, the implementation of *insert* is quite complicated. For the time being we prefer the representation described for a general (unrestricted) sequence in Section 3.2 of this text, together with associated *insert* and *remove* routines equivalent to *insert1* (see Section 3.2.2) and *delete* (see Section 3.2.3). We shall not pursue our study of priority queues at this point.

5.7 Summary of section

A *queue* is a sequence in which a new item can be inserted *only* at the end, or *rear*, of the sequence, and from which the *first* item *only*, at the *front* of the sequence, can be deleted or retrieved. Insertion and deletion operations at the ends of a queue involve no movement of other items and contiguous representation as a static array is an efficient method of implementation. It is desirable to organize the array as an implicit circle. Contiguous representation of a dynamic data structure within a static structure can lead to the problem of *overflow*.

A simulation exercise is presented as an example of a real-world application of queues.

A *priority queue* is a sequence in which the deletion and retrieval operations are applied only to the first item. The order of the items is determined by their relative priorities and the insertion operation preserves the ordering.

Summary of unit

The abstract data type *sequence* is described in detail together with its associated operations: *creation* and *initialization*, *insertion*, *retrieval* and *deletion*. For a general sequence, searching is of fundamental importance to determine where in the sequence to insert a new item and where to find an item which is to be retrieved or deleted. Two special sequences are studied in depth: the *stack* operates on the principle of *last-in-first-out*, i.e. the item to be retrieved or deleted is always the one that was most recently inserted; the *queue* operates on the principle of *first-in-first-out*, i.e. the item to be retrieved or deleted is always the one that has been in the queue the longest. The insertion, retrieval and deletion operations on stacks and queues are much simpler than for general sequences: no searching is necessary.

The number of items in a sequence may vary as a result of insertion and deletion operations. The sequence may be empty and, in theory, it may grow without limit. However, the representation of a (dynamic) sequence as a (static) array or table imposes a limit on the number of items that can be stored. If this limit is exceeded, then *overflow* occurs. This normally results in a fatal execution error. The condition arising from an attempt to retrieve or delete an item from an empty sequence is described as *underflow*. Underflow is not necessarily fatal – recovery may be possible.

A number of example applications of stacks and queues are described. One of the most useful applications of queues is in the simulation of a real-world problem in which demands are made on a time-limited resource. As a result of the simulation, it is possible to gain an understanding of a real-world situation without actually observing its occurrence. The particular application described in this text involves a single server and a single queue.

Looking ahead

In *Unit 3*, we describe a more flexible representation of sequences involving dynamic allocation of storage for new items and the release of that storage when the items are deleted.

Solutions to exercises

Solution 1.1 _____

An array has a predetermined number of elements. Once the array has been created this number of elements cannot be changed. The number of elements in a sequence can vary at runtime.

Solution 3.1 _____

When the sequence has been implemented as a contiguous data structure (e.g. as an array, or a table) and the search requires examination of key field values (on which the sequence is ordered).

Solution 3.2 _____

(i) *codefor*

```
{input} namegiven, sequence

1  set (p) using keysearch (namegiven)
2  if (p = 0) or (item[p].name < > namegiven)
3  then
4     write out 'there is no such name'
5  else
6     set codewanted to item[p].code
7  ifend

{output} codewanted
```

where *keysearch* returns an index to the element at which the search terminates.

(ii) *nameof*

```
{input} codegiven, sequence

set (p) using nonkeysearch (codegiven)
if p = 0
then
    write out 'there is no such code'
else
    set namewanted to item[p].name
ifend

{output} namewanted
```

Solution 3.3 _____

Note that although a value is left in *item*[0].*time* by each insert operation, it is not properly part of the sequence.

After initialization

		time	source
size 0	item 0		
limit 100	1		
	100		

After *insert2* is used for (8.15, Dublin)

		time	source
size 1	0	8.15	
limit 100	1	8.15	Dublin
	2		
	100		

After *insert2* is used for (7.35, Glasgow)

		time	source
size 2	item 0	7.35	
limit 100	1	7.35	Glasgow
	2	8.15	Dublin
	3		
	100		

After *insert2* is used for (9.20, Bristol)

		time	source
size 3	item 0	9.20	
limit 100	1	7.35	Glasgow
	2	8.15	Dublin
	3	9.20	Bristol
	4		
	100		

After *insert2* is used for (7.35, Glasgow)

		time	source
size 4	item 0	7.35	
limit 100	1	7.35	Glasgow
	2	7.35	Glasgow
	3	8.15	Dublin
	4	9.20	Bristol
	5		
	100		

Solution 3.4

Invertifabsent

flight_sequence, timegiven, sourcegiven

1 find where the new item should go in
2 if no identical item is already present
3 then if there is no more room
4   then write out the sequence is full
5   else
6   move all items which should come after the new item down the table by one element;
7   insert the new item;
8   increase the size of the sequence by one.
9   ifend
10 else report item already present
11 ifend

flight_sequence

Solution 3.5

The sequence of states is:

(i) After *sourcedelete* has been applied to *Oslo*

	item	time	source
size 4	0		Oslo
limit 100	1	1.45	Paris
	2	2.05	Rome
	3	3.15	Berlin
	4	3.40	Zurich
	5		
	100		

(ii) After *timedelete* has been applied to *2.05*:

	item	time	source
size 3	0	2.05	
limit 100	1	1.45	Paris
	2	3.15	Berlin
	3	3.40	Zurich
	4		
	100		

After the searching, $p = 2$ and two items have been moved.

(iii) After *sourcedelete* has been applied to *Oslo*, the data structure remains unchanged, except that *Oslo* will be in *item[0].source*. After the search $p = 0$ and no items have been moved.

(iv) After *sourcedelete* has been applied to *Zurich*:

	item	time	source
size 2	0		Zurich
limit 100	1	1.45	Paris
	2	3.15	Berlin
	3		
	100		

After the search, $p = 3$ and no items have been moved.

Solution 4.1

(i) After *initializestack*

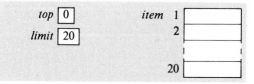

(ii) After pushing *Bill*

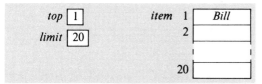

(iii) After pushing *Mary*

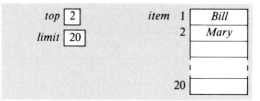

(iv) After popping into *datawanted*

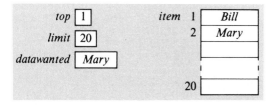

(Note that although *Mary* is still located in *item[2]*, we cannot reference it; the top item of the stack is in *item[1]*.)

(v) After pushing *John*

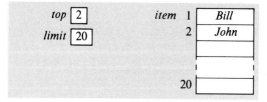

(vi) After pushing *Jim*

top	3		item 1	Bill
limit	20		2	John
			3	Jim
			20	

(iv)

front	3		q	23
rear	1			
size	3			24
maxqueue	4			6

Solution 5.1

When, and only when, the queue is empty before the insertion of the required item.

Solution 5.2

(i)

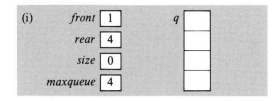

front	1		q	
rear	4			
size	0			
maxqueue	4			

(ii)

front	1		q	17
rear	3			12
size	3			24
maxqueue	4			

(iii)

front	2		q	
rear	3			12
size	2			24
maxqueue	4			

Solution 5.3

(i) The type of *item* field of the record is changed from
array[1..maxqueue] **of** *string* to
array[1..maxqueue] **of** *item_type*.
No other change is required to the data structure.

(ii) No changes are necessary to the routines *initialize* and *empty*.

(iii) In the headings of the procedures *insert* and *remove*, the type specification of the formal parameter *x* is changed from *string* to *item_type*.
No other changes are necessary.

Solution 5.4

(i) *empty* uses values in the queue data structure to determine if the queue is empty; it does not assign new values to any fields of the queue representation so the **var** specification is not required.

(ii) Each of *initialize*, *remove* and *insert* updates the queue by assigning a new value to one or more fields, it is therefore essential that the formal parameter be specified as a **var** parameter, otherwise the corresponding actual parameter will not be updated.

Unit 3 Sequences: Dynamic Storage

Prepared by the Course Team

Contents

Study guide

This unit is shorter than the two preceding units but it introduces entirely new concepts with which you must become thoroughly familiar before proceeding with the remaining units in this block.

Section 2 is the first major section. It introduces two new concepts: the data type pointer and dynamic variables, and then shows their use in the construction of linked sequences based on dynamic storage organization. After this introduction, the section describes in some detail, with diagrammatic illustrations, the implementation of a linked sequence and its associated operations: initialization, retrieval, insertion, deletion and assignment which you met in the previous unit in the context of static storage representations. There is too much material in this section to cover in one evening. Section 3 introduces an application of a linked sequence. We suggest that you allocate two full evenings for the study of Sections 2 and 3 together. You should devote most of this time to Section 2.

The implementation of these concepts in Pascal is described in Section 4. This will be relatively straightforward if you have first mastered Section 2. It is important to work through all the exercises and SAQs in order to become thoroughly familiar with Pascal pointers. This is essential preparation for the main practical activity in the final section. It is well worth spending a full evening on this preparation and possibly running the elementary pointer programs on your computer to convince yourself that they really work as we say they do. Section 4 should take one evening of study time.

The practical exercise in Section 5 is a substantial piece of work involving the application of the programming techniques for handling linked lists, which have been studied in the earlier sections. Time spent in desk checking the design will greatly increase your chances of success when you use the computer. Be prepared to spend up to a couple of hours on the development of your program before testing it on the computer. The whole exercise will take two evenings of study time.

Study plan

Section	Media required	Time
1 Introduction	Text	
2 Linked representation	Text	
3 Undelivered orders problem	Text	2 evenings
4 Pointers in Pascal	Text HCF	1 evening
5 Practical exercise	Text HCF	
6 Epilogue	Text	2 evenings

1 *Introduction*

In the *first* unit of this block we made the distinction between *static data structures*, which, once created, cannot change in size, and *dynamic data structures* in which the number of elements may change as a result of the operations on the data structures. We presented arrays, records and tables as examples of static data structures. The total number of elements (i.e. stored values) of an array is fixed, it cannot be increased by inserting a new element, nor can it be decreased by deleting an element. If we wish to delete the second element of a one-dimensional array so that the third element becomes the second and the fourth becomes the third, and so on, then we can only achieve this by moving the third and successive elements down one position and noting that the last element position is no longer in use. Similarly, to insert a new element, all elements from the point of insertion must be moved up to make room for the insertion. If we underestimate the maximum number of elements which have to be stored in an array, then there is no way of increasing the size of the array at runtime. The array declaration must be changed to increase the number of elements, the program must be recompiled and execution started again from the beginning with the larger array. This is entirely consistent with our definition of a one-dimensional array as

a data structure in which corresponding to each index value *from a predefined fixed range*, there is an item of data of a predefined type.

The important words here are a *predefined fixed range*, emphasizing the *static* nature of an array.

In *Unit 2* we introduced the abstract data type *sequence*

a dynamic data structure having zero or more items of data placed in order according to some predefined relationship.

The surprising thing about a sequence is that it may be empty. All sequences start as empty and their size can vary during program execution as a result of insertion and deletion operations. So far we have not been able to take full advantage of the *dynamic* nature of a sequence because our particular methods of implementation have been constrained by the use of a static data structure (an array) in which to represent the sequence. Thus, insertion in a sequence represented in an array generally requires a number of elements to be moved to make room for the insertion, and deletion of an item leaves a gap which must be closed by moving items. Furthermore, the insertion operation will result in overflow if the capacity of the static array is exceeded.

All these problems are associated with the use of static storage structures. They can be overcome by our second method of representation, which is described in this unit, but, as you will see, the increased flexibility is not without cost!

2 *Linked representation*

Linked representation is our second method for representing a sequence and implementing the operations on it. Linked representation involves the following:

(i) The items which form the sequence are not necessarily held in contiguous storage locations in the order in which they occur in the sequence.

(ii) Each item has an *additional* field, called a **link**, which is used to reference the next item in the sequence.

(iii) The link field in the last item indicates, in some appropriate way, that there are no further items.

(iv) Associated with the sequence is a variable (external to the list) which points to, and thus contains the address of, the *first item in the sequence*. We call this variable a *pointer variable*.

Note that an item in this context is *not* an elementary data item but a composite data item represented as a record having one or more data fields and a link field. We shall use the words item and record interchangeably in this unit.

Thus Figure 2.1 shows the same sequence of records as in *Unit 2* of this block.

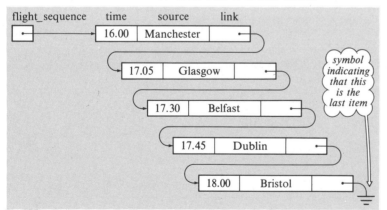

Figure 2.1 *A sequence of linked records*

2.1 Pointer variables

Pointer variables and operations on pointers are of fundamental importance and are central to this unit and the following two units in this block. We shall, therefore, begin by introducing the abstract data type *pointer* and then show, in more detail, how pointers are used in the representation of sequences.

A variable of type **pointer** is a variable which can contain a pointer or reference to another variable. Figure 2.2 shows how we shall represent pointers diagrammatically. This figure also introduces some naming conventions associated with pointers. Here *name* identifies a pointer variable whose *value* is a pointer to another variable. This *second* variable is denoted by *name^* (i.e. the pointer variable followed by a circumflex accent) and it is the variable to which *name* points.

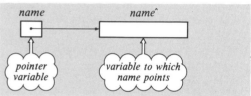

Figure 2.2

In order to give you a mental image of a pointer variable we ask you to picture the memory of some hypothetical computer as a number of consecutive storage locations. We shall number these locations #0, #1, #2, #3, ... (The symbol # serves to distinguish a numerical address value from an ordinary integer. This distinction is important because some operations associated with integers, e.g. multiplication and division, have no meaning in the context of addresses.)

We can picture the memory as shown in Figure 2.3 and can refer to any individual location by its address.

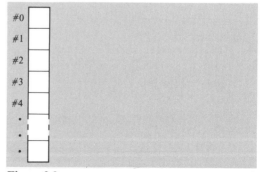

Figure 2.3

With this model, suppose the records for Manchester and Glasgow (in Figure 2.1) are stored at #100 and #150, and that the variable *flight_sequence* is stored at #20. Then this situation is represented as shown in Figure 2.4.

In terms of this model, the value of a pointer variable is the address of the variable to which the pointer variable points.

Thus, *flight_sequence* is a pointer variable which points to the first item in the sequence; its value is #100, the address of the record for Manchester. Similarly, the link field of the Manchester record is a pointer variable which points to the next item in the sequence. Its value is #150, the address of the Glasgow record. The link field of the Glasgow record is a pointer variable which contains the address of the next record in the sequence, and so on, until we come to the end of the sequence. We need some way of denoting that the link field of the last item is special—it has no next item to point to, so the value of this pointer variable has to be immediately recognizable as 'not an address'; we say it is a *nil* pointer. *nil* is represented diagrammatically as shown in the Bristol record of Figure 2.1.

We have said that the items which form a sequence are not necessarily held in contiguous storage locations in the order in which they occur in the sequence. Suppose that each item of the sequence of flight records in Figure 2.1 requires 15 units of storage and that items are stored sequentially, starting at location #101, with one item occupying storage locations #101 to #115, another occupying #116 to #130, and so on. The items are to be linked together in increasing order of the *time* field to represent the sequence of Figure 2.1. Figure 2.5 shows how this is done.

The first item of the sequence (the Manchester record) is located at address #131 so the pointer value to be assigned to the external pointer *flight_sequence* is #131. The link field of the Manchester record must point to the Glasgow record, which is located at #101, so #101 is assigned to the link field of the Manchester record. The Glasgow record, in turn, points to the Belfast record, located at #161, and so on to the end of the sequence. The

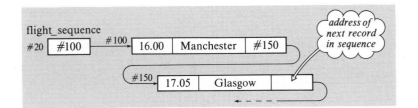

Figure 2.5

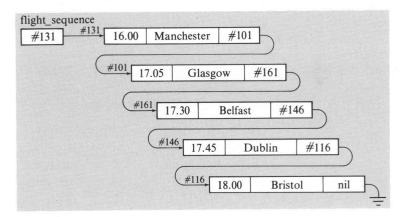

Figure 2.6

Bristol record doesn't point anywhere. We represent this by writing the special pointer value *nil* in its link field. The result is the linked sequence shown in Figure 2.6, drawn in the style of Figure 2.1 but with actual pointer values written in the link fields.

SAQ 2.1

For the items of the *flight_sequence* located as in Figure 2.5, write new pointer values into the link fields to represent the sequence with items ordered alphabetically on the *source* field. Show the result as

(a) a diagram in the style of Figure 2.6, and

(b) a diagram in the style of Figure 2.5.

6

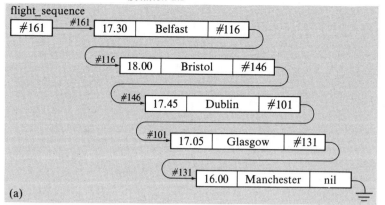

Solution 2.1

(a)

Figure 2.7

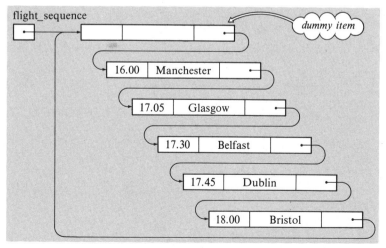

(b)

#101	17.05	Glasgow	#131
#116	18.00	Bristol	#146
#131	16.00	Manchester	nil
#146	17.45	Dublin	#101
#161	17.30	Belfast	#116

flight_sequence

Figure 2.8

Note that the items themselves have not been moved to obtain the new order; only the pointer values in the link fields have changed.

You may have gained the impression that the programmer who uses pointer variables has to know precisely where each variable is stored in the memory and is responsible for manipulating actual addresses. Fortunately, this is not so. When we describe the Pascal implementation of pointers you will see that such details are hidden from the user. From now on we

Figure 2.9 *A linked representation of the sequence from Figure 1.1, including a dummy item*

shall not normally refer explicitly to the actual addresses of items but shall simply use arrows, representing pointers, in diagrammatic illustrations of linked data structures.

Experience has shown that it is often beneficial to include one extra **dummy item** in the sequence as shown in Figure 2.9 and to have:

- the pointer variable (*flight_sequence* in this example) always pointing to the dummy item and thus locating the start of the sequence;
- the link field in the last item in the sequence always pointing back to the dummy item.

No specific values are assigned to the data fields of a dummy item, but as you will see, we shall find a use for them when searching a list. For the present we shall use only the link field of the dummy item.

One result of using a dummy item is that an empty sequence is represented as in Figure 2.10, i.e. as a sequence containing just the dummy item.

Figure 2.10 *The empty sequence*

The presence of the dummy item simplifies many operations on the sequence, by providing a location which can be used in much the same way as the dummy item, *item*[0], in our contiguous representation of a sequence. We shall assume that the dummy item has the same structure as other items in the sequence but only its link field is used. No specific values are assigned to the data fields *source* and *time*.

SAQ 2.2

What is the purpose of the link field in the linked representation of a sequence?

Solution 2.2

The link field is used to point either to the next item in the sequence or, if it is itself in the last item, to the dummy item at the start of the sequence.

Exercise 2.1

Draw, in the style of Figure 2.9, the linked representation of the sequence shown in Figure 2.11. The sequence is ordered chronologically by date.

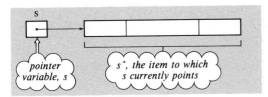

Figure 2.11

We have already introduced a notation for referring to the item to which a pointer variable refers. If *s* is a pointer variable and has been assigned a pointer to some item, then we refer to that item as *s*ˆ. In other words, *s*ˆ is the item to which *s* points in Figure 2.12.

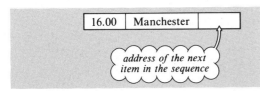

Figure 2.12

In Figure 2.1, the variable *flight_sequence* is a pointer variable. *flight_sequence*ˆ, the item to which *flight_sequence* points, is shown in Figure 2.13.

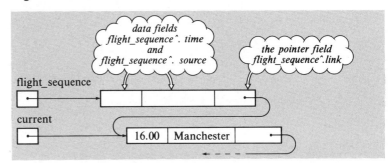

Figure 2.13

Generally, the items in a linked sequence have two or more fields, including the link field, and are represented as records. Using the familiar notation for referring to a field of a record,

> flight_sequenceˆ.source

has the value Manchester, and

> flight_sequenceˆ.time

has the value 16.00.

If *current* is a pointer variable of the same type as *flight_sequence* we may write

> set current to flight_sequence

This sets the value of *current* to *flight_sequence*. Similarly, we may write

> set current to flight_sequenceˆ.link

Let us pause for a while and consider what this means.

*flight_sequence*ˆ is the item to which *flight_sequence* points, i.e. the first item in our flight sequence.

*flight_sequence*ˆ.*link* is the *link* field of that first item, which contains a pointer to the second item. Thus,

> set current to flight_sequenceˆ.link

sets *current* to the pointer value contained in the link field of the first item in the flight sequence. The result of this assignment is that *current* then points to the second item of the flight sequence as shown in Figure 2.14.

Figure 2.14 *The result of assigning flight_sequenceˆ.link to current*

If *current* now points to the second item of the flight sequence, what is the result of the following assignment statement?

> set current to currentˆ.link

*current*ˆ denotes the item to which *current* points (the second item of the sequence) so the value of *current*ˆ.*link* is the value held in the link field of the second item, which is a pointer to the third item. The result of the assignment is, therefore, to make *current* point to the third item in the sequence. This gives a clue as to how we can access items in a linked sequence: in general, if *current* points to an item in a linked sequence, then the assignment 'set current to currentˆ.link' makes *current* point to the next item in the sequence.

SAQ 2.3

For the sequence and the pointer values shown in Figure 2.15 (overleaf),

(i) what is the result of the following assignment?

> set current to currentˆ.link

(ii) what then is the value of

(a) *current*ˆ.*time*, and
(b) *current*ˆ.*source*?

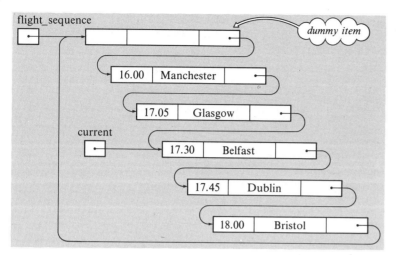

Figure 2.15

Solution 2.3

(i) *current*ˆ is the record containing (17.30, Belfast) so *current*ˆ.*link* is the address stored in the link field of this record, i.e. the address of the next record in the sequence. After the assignment *current* points to the record for Dublin.

(ii) (a) *current*ˆ.*time* then has the value 17.45 and

(b) *current*ˆ.*source* has the value Dublin.

SAQ 2.4 _____

For a linked sequence, *s*, of records having the general structure shown in Figure 2.16, produce a program design to locate the last item in the sequence, i.e. the item whose link field points back to the dummy item.

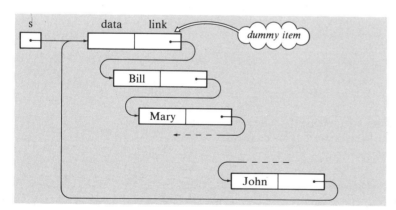

Figure 2.16

Solution 2.4

```
1  set current to point to the dummy item
2  loop while the link field of current item does not point to dummy
                                                                  item
3      move current to the next item in the sequence
4  loopend
```

Figure 2.17

On exit from the loop in Figure 2.17, if the current item is the dummy item, then the dummy item points to itself, so the sequence is empty (see Figure 2.10). Otherwise, the current item is the last item in the sequence; its link field points back to the dummy item.

Now let us refine this design. We shall use a pointer variable, *current*, as we move through the sequence. *s*ˆ is the dummy item, so initially *current* is set to *s* and we can refine the design as shown in Figure 2.18.

```
1.1  set current to s
2.1  loop while current ˆ.link < > s
3.1      set current to current ˆ.link
4.   loopend
```

Figure 2.18

On exit *current*ˆ.*link* = *s* and *current* points to the last item in the sequence. If *current* = *s* then the sequence is empty and *current* points to the dummy item.

Exercise 2.2 _____

For the linked sequence *s* shown in Figure 2.16, produce a program design to count the number of items in the sequence.

Exercise 2.3 _____

Still using the sequence *s* in Figure 2.16, write down, in pointer notation, the steps involved in retrieving the data value from the first item (following the dummy item) in the sequence.

2.2 Storage management

We are almost ready to examine the implementation of a range of operations on a linked representation of a sequence. But there is a fundamental question that must be answered before we can proceed. Sequences are 'flexible' data structures; we do not declare their size before we start (as with arrays) so items must be created dynamically, i.e. during program execution, as we need them. We have said that all sequences start as empty and that their size increases as new items are inserted. The question is where do we get the storage locations to hold the new values? Also, when an item is deleted from a sequence and is no longer required, what happens to the storage space previously occupied by that item? Clearly, we need a storage management system which provides us with the facility to *get* space for a new item whenever we need it and to return that space when it is no longer required. It is convenient to think in terms of a pool of available storage locations which are allocated on demand; when a location is no longer required, it is returned to the pool.

Two basic modules are required to allocate space to new items and to reclaim that space when it is no longer required.

The module *getspace* allocates space. The statement:

> set (p) using getspace ( )

uses the storage management system to allocate space to hold a new uninitialized record and sets the pointer variable *p* to point to this newly created record.

The module *freespace* reclaims unwanted space. The statement:

> set ( ) using freespace (p)

releases the space currently allocated to the dynamic variable to which *p* refers. The space so released is returned to the pool of free space and is then available for reallocation, using *getspace*, as and when required.

With this notion of available space we are now ready to consider operations on linked representations of sequences. [For brevity, we shall normally refer to a *linked representation of a sequence* as a *linked sequence*.]

2.3 Operations on a linked sequence

2.3.1 Initialization

Having assumed the existence of a pool of items which can be drawn upon when we want a new item, and which is also used to receive disposed of items which are no longer needed, we now consider some operations on a linked sequence. The first of these is initialization.

As explained earlier, an empty sequence is implemented as shown in Figure 2.10. So, in order to initialize a sequence *s*, we:

> 1 get an item from the pool and make s point to it
> 2 make the link field of the item point to the item itself

This can be implemented as a module *init_sequence* as shown in Figure 2.19.

init_sequence

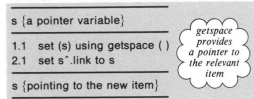

Figure 2.19

The resulting empty sequence is shown in Figure 2.20.

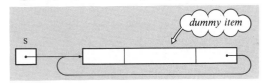

Figure 2.20 *A sequence which has just been initialized*

2.3.2 Retrieval

As in the previous unit, we shall study some processes for retrieving information, before we look at the operations of insertion and deletion. This is because the operation of retrieval involves searching, and the same searching will be useful when we come later to insert and delete items.

We can use *only* linear searching techniques on a linked sequence. The faster binary search cannot now be applied, because the items in the sequence are not in contiguous storage locations and therefore, cannot be accessed by indexing. To find a specified item we must simply start at the beginning of the sequence and follow the link fields, looking at each item in turn.

We start by trying to find an item in a sequence with a given value in its key field. In our flight sequence example the items are ordered with the time field as the key. We accordingly:

> 1 Place the given time in s^.time (i.e. in the time field of the dummy item of sequence s)
> 2 Start the search at the first item in the sequence
> 3 Search forward through the sequence for an item, q^, with a time greater than or equal to the given time

For example, given a search module, *keysearch1*, which we use to look for *timegiven = 17.45* in the sequence of Figure 2.9, but with *s* in place of *flight_sequence*, then the pointer *q* will be set as shown in Figure 2.21.

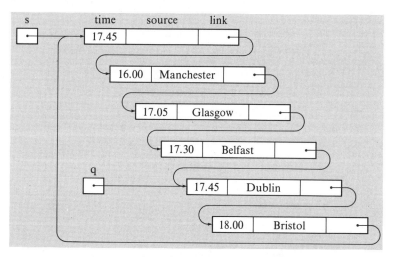

Figure 2.21 *The sequence after the execution of keysearch1, looking for timegiven = 17.45*

This process can be described more formally as a module as shown in Figure 2.22.

keysearch1

timegiven, s
1.1 set sˆ.time to timegiven 2.1 set q to sˆ.link 3.1 loop while qˆ.time < timegiven 3.2   set q to qˆ.link 3.3 loopend
q {a pointer to an item with   qˆ.time > = timegiven}

Figure 2.22

Had we executed the module *keysearch1*, looking for *timegiven = 17.20* the value returned would have been *q* pointing to (17.30, Belfast), which, since *qˆ.time > 17.20*, tells us that no item in the sequence has a time field whose value is equal to *timegiven*.

Again, had we executed *keysearch1*, looking for *timegiven = 18.30*, the value returned would be *q = s* since the search is terminated by finding the value 18.30, which was placed in the dummy item. This indicates once again that the required time was not present.

The corresponding search process to find an item in a sequence, using its value in a *nonkey* field, i.e. the *source* field in our example, can be implemented as shown in the module in Figure 2.23.

nonkeysearch1

sourcegiven, s
1.1 set sˆ.source to sourcegiven 2.1 set q to sˆ.link 3.1 loop while qˆ.source < > sourcegiven 3.2   set q to qˆ.link 3.3 loopend
q {a pointer to an item with   qˆ.source = sourcegiven}

Figure 2.23

In this case the only condition for terminating the search is:
qˆ.source = sourcegiven. So the process always find either an item with the given source, or the dummy item in which the given source has been placed.

Exercise 2.4

What would be the values of *qˆ.time* and *qˆ.source* as a result of executing the following operations on the sequence in Figure 2.9?

(i)   *keysearch1*, looking for 17.30.
(ii) *keysearch1*, looking for 16.30.
(iii) *nonkeysearch1*, looking for Dublin.
(iv) *nonkeysearch1*, looking for Edinburgh.

The extension of these search processes into modules which will:

(i) Find a source, given a time, or
(ii) Find a time, given a source

is similar to the method we used in the previous unit—we need to use the pointer resulting from the search either to find the required data or to report its absence. In detail the results are as shown in Figures 2.24 and 2.25.

sourceof

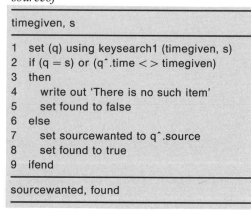

timegiven, s
1 set (q) using keysearch1 (timegiven, s) 2 if (q = s) or (qˆ.time < > timegiven) 3 then 4   write out 'There is no such item' 5   set found to false 6 else 7   set sourcewanted to qˆ.source 8   set found to true 9 ifend
sourcewanted, found

Figure 2.24

timefor

sourcegiven, s
1   set (q) using nonkeysearch1 (sourcegiven, s)
2   if q = s
3   then
4   write out 'There is no such source'
5   set found to false
6   else
7   set timewanted to qˆ.time
8   set found to true
9   ifend
timewanted, found

Figure 2.25

2.3.3 Insertion

One of the main advantages of a linked representation is that new items can be inserted in the sequence without moving any of the existing items. We merely have to get an item from the pool, place the appropriate data in it and link it into the existing sequence at the correct place. Thus, a design for the required process is:

1   get an item from the pool
2   place the data in it
3   find where the new item should go in
4   link the item into the sequence

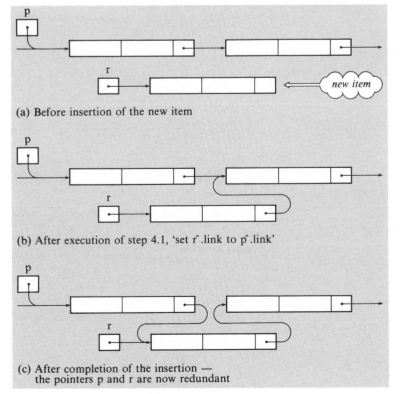

(a) Before insertion of the new item

(b) After execution of step 4.1, 'set rˆ.link to pˆ.link'

(c) After completion of the insertion —
    the pointers p and r are now redundant

Figure 2.26

The process of linking the new item into the sequence is illustrated in Figure 2.26. The pointer variable p points to the item *after* which the insertion is to be made. r points to the new item which has been obtained from the pool and in which the given data has been placed.

We make the link field of the new item point to the item which is to follow it in the sequence, i.e. to the item whose address is in pˆ.*link*. This is performed by the design statement

> 4.1   set rˆ.link to pˆ.link — see Figure 2.26(b)

Then we assign the address of the new item (contained in the variable r) to the link field of pˆ with the statement

> 4.2   set pˆ.link to r   —   see Figure 2.26(c)

This completes the insertion.

Let us assume that the sequence is ordered on a *key* field (e.g. the time field in our *flight_sequence*) then the search for the point at which to make the insertion can be similar to *keysearch1*. To find the place for the new item it is necessary to use a version of *keysearch1* (Figure 2.22) which sets a pointer, p, pointing to the item *after* which the new item must go. The appropriate module is shown in Figure 2.27.

keysearch2

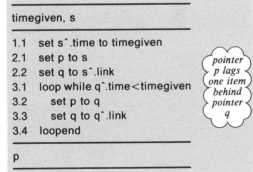

timegiven, s	
1.1 set sˆ.time to timegiven	
2.1 set p to s	
2.2 set q to sˆ.link	
3.1 loop while qˆ.time<timegiven	*pointer p lags one item behind pointer q*
3.2 set p to q	
3.3 set q to qˆ.link	
3.4 loopend	
p	

Figure 2.27

Notice that in this design, the pointer p trails behind the pointer q, that is, p and q always point to successive items in the sequence as illustrated in Figure 2.28.

Exercise 2.5

What would be the result of *keysearch2* if *timegiven* were already present in the sequence?

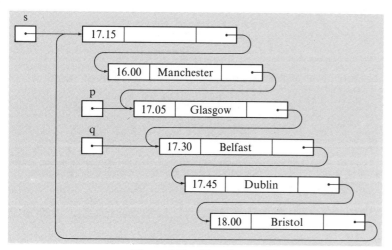

Figure 2.28 *After the searching stage of an insertion*

A call to *keysearch2* is the third step in the *insert* module of Figure 2.29.

insert

---

timegiven, sourcegiven, s

1.1 set (r) using getspace ( )
 {place data in new item}
2.1 set r^.time to timegiven
2.2 set r^.source to sourcegiven
3.1 set (p) using keysearch2 (timegiven, s)
 {link the new item into the sequence}
4.1 set r^.link to p^.link
 {adjust pointer of predecessor record}
4.2 set p^.link to r

---

s {with the additional item inserted}

---

r is a local pointer variable of the same type as p. It points to the new item

Figure 2.29

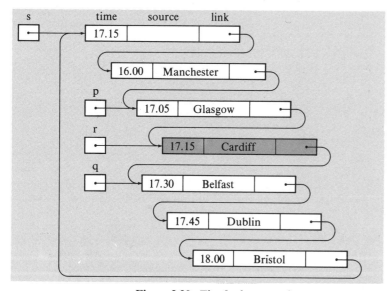

Figure 2.30 *The final stages of an insertion*

Suppose for example, that we need to insert (17.15, Cardiff) in the sequence in Figure 2.9. After the execution of *keysearch2*, looking for *timegiven = 17.15*, the state of the structure will be as shown in Figure 2.28.

The remaining steps get a new item, make *r* point to it, and then link it into the sequence. The final state is shown in Figure 2.30. Note that the pointers *p*, *q* and *r* are now redundant.

This insertion process would work equally well if the sequence had been initially empty (i.e. with just the dummy item in it).

Exercise 2.6

Given the empty sequence of flights in Figure 2.31, draw similar diagrams to show the state after each of the following successive operations:

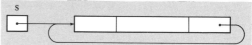

Figure 2.31

(i) Insert the item (2.30, Rome).
(ii) Insert the item (4.10, Oslo).
(iii) Insert the item (3.30, Berlin).

Show also the state of *p* and *r* immediately before leaving the module *insert*.

2.3.4 Deletion

As with insertion, a linked representation enables us to avoid moving the items when one of them is deleted. An appropriate design of the process is shown in Figure 2.32.

1 search for the item to be deleted
2 if it is not present
3 then
4   report that no such item exists
5 else
6   delete the item
7   return the deleted item to the pool
8 ifend

Figure 2.32

Two versions of a suitable delete routine, *timedelete* and *sourcedelete*, are shown in Figures 2.33 and 2.34.

timedelete is to be used when the item to be deleted is defined by its *time* field (the *key* field) and *sourcedelete* when it is determined by its *source* field (the *nonkey* field). The only difference between the two routines lies *timedelete*

timegiven, s
1.1 set (p) using keysearch2 (timegiven, s)
2.1 set q to pˆ.link
2.2 if (q = s) or (qˆ.time < > timegiven)
3 then
4.1   write out 'Error, no such time present'
5 else
6.1   set pˆ.link to qˆ.link
7.1   set ( ) using freespace (q)
{return space to storage pool}
8 ifend
s {with item deleted}

Figure 2.33

sourcedelete

sourcegiven, s
1.1 set (p) using nonkeysearch2 (sourcegiven, s)
2.1 set q to pˆ.link
2.2 if q = s
3 then
4.1   write out 'Error, no such source present'
5 else
6.1   set pˆ.link to qˆ.link
7.1   set ( ) using freespace (q)
{return space to storage pool}
8 ifend
s {with item deleted}

Figure 2.34

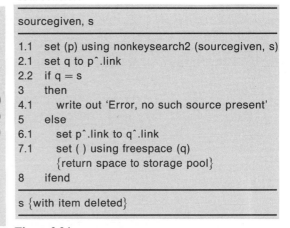

q is a local pointer variable of the same type as p. It points to the item to be deleted

in the searching process: *timedelete* uses *keysearch2*, the process used in *insert*; while *sourcedelete* uses *nonkeysearch2*, which is simply a version of *nonkeysearch1* which sets up a pointer to the item preceding the item which is to be deleted.

We saw in the previous section that to insert an item we must assign its address to the link field of its predecessor in the sequence. Similarly, to delete an item we must change the value of the link field of the preceding item.

An application of these routines is illustrated in Figures 2.35 and 2.36.

They show what will occur if we execute

either   *timedelete*, looking for *17.30*

or   *sourcedelete*, looking for *Belfast*.

In both cases the searching process leaves *p* pointing to the item preceding that to be deleted. *q* is then set to point to the item to be deleted. The link field in *p*ˆ is changed, so that *q*ˆ is removed from the sequence, and *freespace(q)* then puts the space used by the item referenced by *q* back in the pool.

SAQ 2.5 _____

What is the main advantage of the linked representation of a sequence?

Solution 2.5

New items can be inserted (preserving order) and deletions made, without moving any of the existing items.

SAQ 2.6 _____

What is the main disadvantage of the linked representation of a sequence?

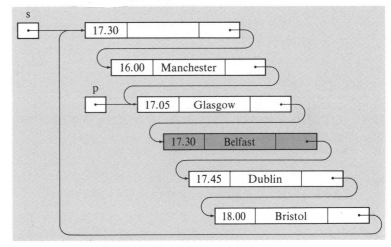

Figure 2.35 *After the searching stage of deletion*

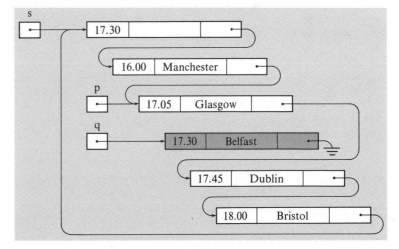

Figure 2.36 *After completion of the deletion*

Solution 2.6

Searching must be done sequentially; individual items cannot be indexed so a binary search cannot be applied.

Exercise 2.7 _____

Given the sequence as it appears at the end of Exercise 2.6, show its state after each of the following operations:

(i)   *timedelete*, looking for 2.30.
(ii) *sourcedelete*, looking for Berlin.
(iii) *timedelete*, looking for 3.30.
(iv) *sourcedelete*, looking for Oslo.

2.3.5 Assignment

Consider the implementation of an operation to construct a new sequence *s1* with the same value as an existing sequence *s*, i.e. *s1* is to be a copy of *s*. We regard this as implementing the assignment operation

set (s1) to copy of (s)

A design for this is shown in Figure 2.37.

This is implemented by the module in

```
1   initialize an empty sequence s1
2   set current to point to the item following the dummy item of s
3   loop while current is not at the dummy item in s
4       get a new item from the pool of available space
5       copy the data from the current item in s into the new item
6       link the new item into the end of sequence s1
7       move current to the next item in s
8   loopend
9   make the last item in s1 point to the dummy item of s1
```

Figure 2.37

copy
_____

s {pointer to sequence to be copied}
_____

```
        {create a new sequence, s1, initially empty}
1.1     set (s1) using init_sequence ( )
        {mark the end of the new sequence}
1.2     set end_of_s1 to s1
        {copying starts with first item of sequence s}
2.1     set current to s^.link
3.1     loop while current < > s
            {get space for copy of current item}
4.1         set (r) using getspace ( )
            {copy data from current item of s to newly created item}
5.1         set r^.data to current^.data
            {link new item to end of s1}
6.1         set end_of_s1^.link to r
            {adjust end_of_s1}
6.2         set end_of_s1 to r
            {advance current to next item of s}
7.1         set current to current^.link
8       loopend
        {link end_of_s1 back to s1}
9.1     set end_of_s1^.link to s1
```
_____

s1 {a new sequence of values copied from s}
_____

Figure 2.38

Figure 2.38. Notice that we have assumed an item with a single data field and link field. The generalization to several data fields is straightforward. The module uses the local pointer variables *r* and *current*; *r* moves through the new list, while *current* moves through the list to be copied. Also, there is a variable *end_of_s1* which always points to the last item in the list *s1*. (Its link field points to the dummy item.)

Exercise 2.8 _____

(i) Draw in the style of this unit the linked sequence, *s*, of names Bill, Mary, Jane, in that order (i.e. the order of the sequence is the order in which the data was input). Show in your diagram the effect of the pointer assignment 'set *s1* to *s*', where *s1* is a pointer variable of the same type as *s*.
(ii) Use the module *copy* to construct a new linked sequence *s1* which is a copy of the sequence *s*; draw diagrams to show the state of *s1* and the pointer variables *end_of_s1*, *current* and *r* on entry to the loop and after each element of *s* has been copied.

2.4 Summary of section

A pointer variable is introduced as a variable capable of holding the address of a data object. The linked representation of a sequence uses a pointer field in each item to refer to the next item (if any) in the sequence.

The first item in the sequence is referred to by an external pointer variable. The link field of the last item in a sequence may contain a nil value to mark the end of the sequence. However, some operations on a sequence are simplified if the first item in the sequence is a dummy item and the last item points back to this dummy. With this representation, an empty sequence consists of a dummy item which points back to itself.

The standard operations: initialization, searching, retrieval, insertion, deletion and assignment (i.e. copying) and modules to implement them for a linked sequence are described using pointer notation.

A dynamic variable is one for which space is allocated during execution of a program. This space may be released and returned to a pool of available space when the dynamic variable is no longer required. Two modules *getspace* and *freespace* are required to allocate space to a dynamic variable and to reclaim that space when the dynamic variable is no longer required.

3 *The undelivered order problem*

In the warehouse problem of *Unit IV.1* you encountered the question of what to do when an order cannot be fully met from stock. The solution was to send the actual quantity in stock to the customer and to record the rest in a list of all those orders which have not yet been fulfilled. It is company policy to satisfy the longest outstanding orders first, so a sequence of outstanding orders, held in order of date of receipt of the customer orders, is useful. This minimizes the searching necessary when a further delivery of goods is received.

3.1 The unfulfilled order list

Suppose that the unfulfilled order list, *l*, currently has four items in it, as shown in Figure 3.1. For this situation, if 50 television sets are delivered, 15 will be sent to Jones, his record will be deleted from the list and 35 will be placed in the warehouse. If 40 radios are delivered, 26 will be sent to Timms, his record will be deleted, 14 will be sent to Davis and his record updated in the unfulfilled order list.

Exercise 3.1 _____
(i) Draw the unfulfilled order list (of Figure 3.1) as a cyclic linked sequence with a dummy item at its head.
(ii) Show the state of the linked sequence of unfulfilled orders after processing a delivery of:
  (a) 50 television sets,
  (b) 40 radios.

3.2 Insertion in the unfulfilled order list

So much for what happens when a delivery occurs. But how do items get onto the unfulfilled order list in the first place? Clearly, whenever an order is received from a customer a check must be made on whether or not sufficient stock is held in the warehouse to satisfy that order. If there is insufficient stock to meet the order, then an unfulfilled order note is generated,

Customer	Product	Amount	Date of Order
Wilson	Razor	40	88/02/02
Jones	Television	15	88/03/10
Timms	Radio	26	88/03/18
Davis	Radio	34	88/03/21

Figure 3.1

containing data about the order: the name of the customer, the name of the product which is out of stock, the quantity still required to fill the order, and the date of receipt of the order. This new record will be added at the end (i.e. the rear) to maintain the date order of the sequence.

Insertion at the end of a linked sequence in which the last item points back to the dummy item is a special case which can be performed by an efficient technique involving no searching. Suppose the sequence is as shown in the solution to Exercise 3.1 and that there is a new outstanding order for Roberts for 3 fridges on 01 04 88, to be added to the sequence. The special insertion technique, illustrated in Figure 3.2, is as follows:

1. Insert the new item *after* the dummy item (i.e. at the *front* of the sequence)
2. Copy the new data from this new item into the dummy item
3. Move the sequence pointer to point to the new item (which becomes the new dummy item).

The fact that the unfulfilled order sequence is cyclic, i.e. the last record in the sequence links back to the dummy record, enables us to use a device which can save a lot of processing time. Instead of following all the links from the dummy record to the end of the sequence, to add in the new record we can use the dummy record to receive the data of the additional record and then make the new record (inserted after the dummy) the new dummy.

We have looked briefly at the operations of deletion, updating and insertion of records in the unfulfilled order sequence. In a commercially available order processing program, other situations would have to be dealt with. How, for example, would you deal with records on the unfulfilled orders sequence for products no longer manufactured? We shall return to this later, but first we shall describe how pointers are implemented in Pascal.

3.3 Summary of section

The warehouse problem of *Unit IV.1* is revisited and the organization of a list of unfulfilled orders is considered. The list is represented as a linked sequence of records with a dummy record at its head and with the link field of the last record pointing back to the dummy. The operations of deletion, updating and insertion of orders in the list are briefly described.

Figure 3.2*

* We have previously drawn representations of linked sequences with the dummy item at the top of the diagram. In Figure 3.2 the dummy item is shown at the bottom, which, since the representation is cyclic, is equally acceptable and in this case simplifies the illustration of the insertion of a new item.

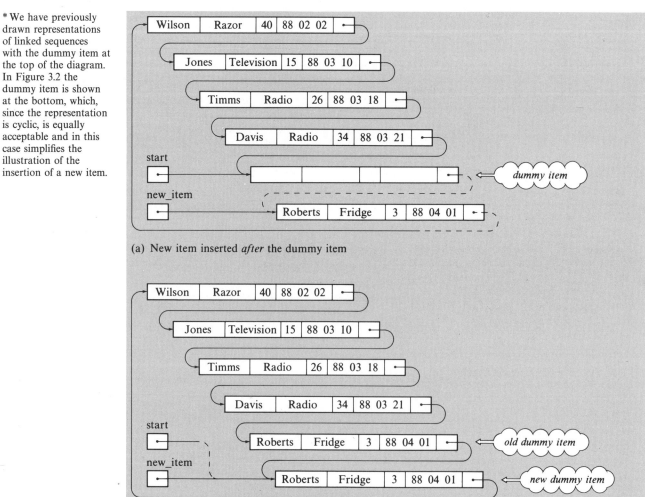

(a) New item inserted *after* the dummy item

(b) Sequence after completion of the insertion.

4 *Pointers in Pascal*

Pascal provides a facility for manipulating pointers and for building data structures using pointers. The notation used is the one we have adopted in the preceding sections. Thus, in Pascal

$p\hat{}$ denotes the data object pointed to by p

and

$q\hat{}$ denotes the data object pointed to by q.

In Pascal, when defining a pointer type, we *must* specify the type of variable to which the pointer points. Specifically,

```
type
    integer_ptr = ^integer;
```

defines the type *integer_ptr* as a pointer to a variable of type *integer*, and

```
type
    real_ptr = ^real;
```

defines the *real_ptr* as a pointer type that refers to a variable of type *real*.

Note that in this context the circumflex is written *before* the type to which it refers. This is read as *pointer to an integer* or *pointer to a real*. When we write the circumflex *after* a (pointer) variable name, such as $p\hat{}$, we read this as the *variable to which p points*.

If we then declare two variables *pi* and *pr* by

```
var
    pi : integer_ptr;
    pr : real_ptr;
```

then the values that can be assigned to *pi* and *pr* will both be addresses (i.e. pointers) but the value of *pi* must be the address of a location containing an *integer* value, while the value of *pr* must be the address at which a value of type *real* is stored. Any attempt to assign the address of an integer to *pr*, for example, is an error.

Given the definitions and declarations above, the constructs *pi*^ and *pr*^ refer to the variables of type *integer* and *real*, respectively. We say:

  pi^ is the variable to which *pi* points
  pr^ is the variable to which *pr* points.

The statement

```
pi^ := 6
```

is executed in two phases. First the value of *pi* is used to access the integer variable *pi*^ (see Figure 4.1(a)), and second, the value of that variable is set to 6 (see Figure 4.1(b)).

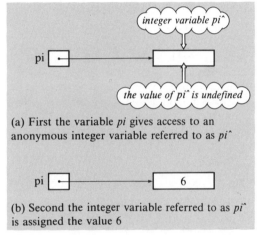

(a) First the variable *pi* gives access to an anonymous integer variable referred to as *pi*^

(b) Second the integer variable referred to as *pi*^ is assigned the value 6

Figure 4.1 *Assignment to a referenced variable*

Similarly the statement

```
write(pi^)
```

first uses the value of *pi* to access the integer variable *pi*^, and then the value contained in that variable is printed.

Note that the statement

```
pi := 6
```

is illegal. *pi* is *not* an integer variable, but a pointer to an integer variable, so it *cannot* be given an integer value.

Similarly,

```
write(pi)
```

is illegal. The value of *pi* is a pointer (that is, an address) and it *cannot* be printed.

The sole purpose of a pointer variable is to provide access to the variable to which it points. This is illustrated in Figure 4.2

18

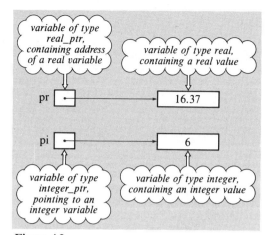

Figure 4.2

4.1 Allocating dynamic variables

Once a variable, *p*, has been declared as a pointer to a specific type of object it must be possible to create an object of the specific type and assign its address to *p*. For example, the declaration

var *pi : integer_ptr;*

when processed, causes a pointer variable *pi* to be created, but, at this stage, *pi* has not been assigned a value; there is no variable for it to point to (see Figure 4.1(a)). So how is the address of an integer variable assigned to *pi*? This may be done in Pascal using a procedure called *new*, which implements the module *getspace* introduced in Section 2.2. We shall not be concerned with how it does so.

Thus, if *p* is a pointer (variable) to an object of some type, the statement

new(p)

creates a variable of that specified type and assigns its address to *p*.

Suppose we are given the type definitions and variable declarations

type
    integer_ptr = ˆinteger;
    real_ptr = ˆreal;
var
    pi : integer_ptr;
    pr : real_ptr;

Initially, the pointer variables *pi* and *pr* have no defined values, but executing the statements

new(pi);
new(pr)

creates the integer variable *pi ˆ* and the real variable *pr ˆ* and assigns their addresses to *pi* and *pr*, respectively.

At this stage the variables *pi ˆ* and *pr ˆ* have no defined values, but executing the statements

pi ˆ := 6;
pr ˆ := 16.37

assigns values to these variables giving the result illustrated in Figure 4.2.

Notice that the pointer variables *pi* and *pr* are created as a result of processing the declarations

var *pi : integer_ptr;*
    pr : real_ptr;

The variables referred to by *pi ˆ* and *pr ˆ* on the other hand are created differently; they are created during execution of the program (*dynamically*) as a result of executing the statements

new(pi);
new(pr)

We say that the variables denoted by *pi ˆ* and *pr ˆ* are dynamic variables; they are created at runtime by executing the procedure *new* with a pointer variable of the appropriate type as its parameter. For brevity we shall write the variable *p ˆ* whenever we want to refer to the dynamic variable pointed to by *p*.

SAQ 4.1

(a) Give a type definition, a variable declaration and executable statements in Pascal to create a dynamic variable *p_char ˆ* containing the character value *'a'*.

(b) Show the result as a diagram in the style of Figure 4.2.

Solution 4.1

(a) **type**
        char_ptr = ˆchar;
    var
        p_char : char_ptr;
    begin
        new(p_char);
        p_char ˆ := 'a';
        :
    end

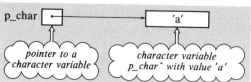

Figure 4.3

```
1   program pointers;
2   var p, q: ^integer;
3   begin
4       new(p);
5       p^ := 3;
6       q := p;
7       writeln(p^, q^)
8   end.
```

Figure 4.4

As a further example of the use of pointers and the procedure *new*, consider the Pascal code in Figure 4.4. First note that instead of using a type definition for a pointer to an *integer*, we have declared *p* and *q* directly as variables of type *^integer* in line 2. This form is equally acceptable to Pascal, although generally we shall use type definitions for pointer types. (You will recall that we used type definitions for array types and record types.) In line 4, a dynamic integer variable *p^* is created and its address assigned to *p*. Line 5 sets the value of that variable to 3. Line 6 then sets the pointer variable *q* to the address of that same integer variable. This is perfectly valid, since the value of one pointer variable, *p*, is being assigned to another pointer variable, *q*.

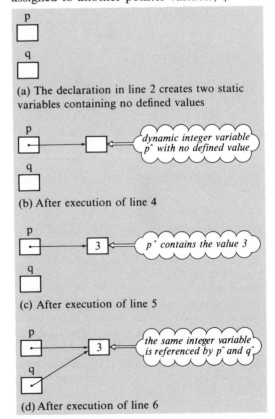

(a) The declaration in line 2 creates two static variables containing no defined values

(b) After execution of line 4

(c) After execution of line 5

(d) After execution of line 6

Figure 4.5 *Steps in the execution of the program in Figure 4.4*

Note that at this point *p^* and *q^* refer to the same integer variable, that is, the variable to which *p* points is also the variable to which *q* points. This is illustrated in Figure 4.5.

Line 7 therefore prints the contents of this variable (which is 3) twice. You may wish to run this simple program on your computer to verify that it really does what we say it does.

```
1   program pointers;
2   var p, q: ^integer;
3       x: integer;
4   begin
5       new(p);
6       p^ := 3;
7       q := p;
8       writeln(p^, q^);
9       x := 7;
10      q^ := x;
11      writeln(p^, q^);
12      new(p);
13      p^ := 5;
14      writeln(p^, q^);
15      p := q;
16      writeln(p^, q^)
17  end.
```

Figure 4.6

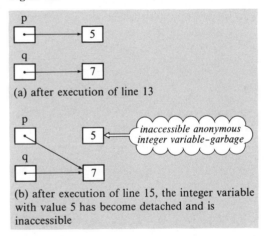

(a) after execution of line 13

(b) after execution of line 15, the integer variable with value 5 has become detached and is inaccessible

Figure 4.7

Now consider the effect of executing the further statements in lines 9 to 11 of Figure 4.6. In line 9 the value of an (ordinary) integer variable *x* is then set to 7, then line 10 changes the value of *q^* to the value of *x*. However, since *p* and *q* both point to the same integer variable *p^* and *q^* both have the value 7. Line 11 therefore prints the value 7 twice.

In line 12 a new dynamic integer variable *p^* is created and then assigned the value 5 (in line 13). This does not affect the value of $q\hat{}$, which is still 7. So line 14 prints the values 5 and 7.

Finally, p is assigned the value of q, so $p\hat{}$ and $q\hat{}$ refer to the same integer variable which has the value 7. Note, however, that the integer variable previously referred to as $p\hat{}$ in line 14 still exists and has value 5, but no variable points to it (see Figure 4.7). We no longer have any access to this 'anonymous' integer variable—it is 'garbage' occupying space which we can no longer use because we don't know its address. The creation of garbage can be a problem in programs which process dynamically created variables. The problem only arises when all the available space has been allocated, i.e. the pool is exhausted. If there is then a further call on the procedure *new* to allocate space for a new item and this request cannot be satisfied then the program cannot proceed. It is sometimes possible to avoid this error situation if space, which has previously been allocated and is no longer in use, can be released.

In this situation the release of space before it becomes inaccessible garbage is recommended. Once garbage is created it cannot be recovered by the Pascal system and cannot be reallocated.

4.2 Freeing dynamic variables

To avoid the problem of garbage the space allocated to a dynamically created variable can be released as soon as you have no further use for it. This is done using the Pascal procedure *dispose* which implements the module *freespace*. Thus, if $p\hat{}$ is a dynamically created variable, then execution of the statement

```
dispose(p)
```

releases the variable $p\hat{}$ and returns the space occupied by it to the pool of free space from which it was originally allocated by the procedure *new*.

Use of the procedure *dispose* can lead to the second major problem associated with the processing of dynamic variables. Consider the fragment of a program in Figure 4.8 where p and q are pointers to *integer* variables.

```
0   new(p);
1   p^ := 3;
2   q := p;
3   dispose(p);
4   writeln(q^)
```

Figure 4.8

On the face of it this is perfectly valid, but let's consider each step in detail:
Line 1 assigns the value 3 to the dynamic variable $p\hat{}$. The address of $p\hat{}$ is then assigned to q in line 2, so $p\hat{}$ and $q\hat{}$ now refer to the *same* variable. In line 3 the variable $p\hat{}$ is released and, having been disposed of, it no longer exists, but $p\hat{}$ and $q\hat{}$ are the same variable, so $q\hat{}$ no longer exists, although q still holds the address of the space previously allocated to $q\hat{}$. The value of q is said to be a *dangling reference*, a pointer to a variable which no longer exists and cannot be accessed. The reference to $q\hat{}$ in line 4 is therefore invalid.

The result of using a dangling reference is unpredictable. It depends on whether the space returned to the pool has been reallocated for another purpose. Debugging can be extremely difficult in this situation. It is not always the case that an error is detected by the system.

It is the programmer's responsibility never to use a dangling pointer in a program.

There is no foolproof way of avoiding dangling references. We can only advise you to take special care, when using *dispose*, to ensure that only one variable points to the object which is about to be released.

4.3 Linked sequences in Pascal

4.3.1 Printing a list of names

In this example we give you a linked list of items and ask you to produce Pascal code (from a given design) to visit each item in the list, from first to last, and print the data contained in that item. In addition to giving you further practice in the manipulation of Pascal pointers we take the opportunity to show the use of a linked sequence which is strictly linear (that is, the last item does not refer back to the first). As the representation is not cyclic we shall need to mark the end of the list with the special nil pointer which we introduced early in this unit (see Figure 2.6). The linked list is illustrated diagrammatically in Figure 4.9.

The process of visiting each item in turn is similar to that used in the solution to Exercise 2.2 but here, instead of counting the items, you must print them. The condition for terminating this process is also different because the representation of the list of names is not cyclic.

Pascal definitions and declarations for the list and its associated pointer variables are given in Figure 4.10.

A top-level design for the process is given in Figure 4.11.

Your task is to refine this design step by step as specified in the following exercises.

Exercise 4.1(a)

The first item referred to in step 1 is the item following the dummy item. Refine step 1 to set the pointer variable *current* to point to this first item and code this step in Pascal.

Exercise 4.1(b)

Write down a Pascal *writeln* statement to print the *info* field of the current item (step 3).

Exercise 4.1(c)

Refine step 4 and code it in Pascal.

All that remains to be refined is step 2.

2   loop while the list is not exhausted

We have assumed that the last node in the list is marked by the special pointer value *nil*, so the list is exhausted when current has the value *nil*. Step 2 is therefore refined as:

2.1   loop while current is not nil

Pascal provides an implementation of the empty pointer *nil* as a special pointer value **nil**. Any pointer variable may be assigned the value **nil** whatever the type of the variable to which that pointer can point.

Thus **nil** may be assigned to pointer variables of **type** ^*integer*, ^*real*, ^*char* and ^*item_type*, where *item_type* is any **type** the user may choose to specify.

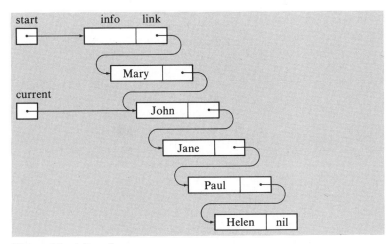

Figure 4.9 *A list of names*

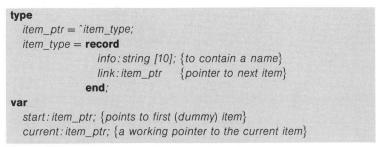

Figure 4.10

1	visit the first item in the list (if any)
2	loop while the list is not exhausted
3	write out the info field of the current item
4	advance to the next item in the list
5	loopend

Figure 4.11

Exercise 4.1(d)

Write down the complete Pascal code to implement steps 2 to 5, using the Pascal pointer value **nil** in your implementation of step 2.

4.3.2 The undelivered orders problem revisited

As a further and more detailed illustration of the use of pointer variables in the construction and processing of a linked sequence, we consider again the undelivered order problem introduced in Section 3. Each order, in the linked list of orders which have not yet been fulfilled, is represented as a record consisting of five fields, the first four of which contain the customer name, the product name, an amount and the date of the order. The fifth field is a link or pointer variable. In addition to the pointer fields in the records in the orders list we use an external pointer variable to the first record in the list (a dummy record). This representation of the orders list is illustrated in Figure 4.12.

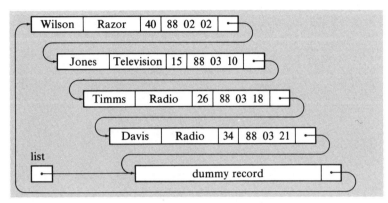

Figure 4.12

We could define the type of the pointer variable, *list*, and of the record to which it points as shown in Figure 4.13.

```
type
    order_ptr = ^order_type;
    order_type = record
                    customer: string[20];
                    product  : string[20];
                    amount   : integer;
                    date     : string[8]; {as yy/mm/dd}
                    link     : order_ptr
                 end;
```

Figure 4.13

A record of such type is identical to the record types introduced in *Unit 1* of this block, except that the link field is a pointer (containing the address of the next record in the list).

Note that in defining *order_ptr* we have referred to the type *order_type* before that type is actually defined. Pascal permits a reference to the type (in this case *order_type*) before that type has been defined. This is because it is unnecessary to know all the details of a variable of that type in order to implement a pointer to it. A pointer is, after all, only an address. The storage requirements for an address are the same

regardless of the object located at that address.

Given the type definitions of Figure 4.13:

(i) Write down a declaration for the external pointer *list* of Figure 4.13

(ii) Write down a statement to create dynamically a dummy order pointed to by *list*

(iii) Write down a reference to the dummy order, and

(iv) Give a Pascal statement to make the link field of the dummy order point to the dummy order itself, so initializing an empty list of orders.

Solution 4.2

(i)   **var** *list : order_ptr;*

(ii)   *new(list)*

(iii) *list ^*

(iv)   *list ^.link := list*

If the pointer variable *p* points to the record for Timms' order (in Figure 4.12):

(i) How would you refer to the product field of this order in Pascal?

(ii) What is the result of executing the following statement?

```
p := p^.link
```

(iii) Write down the value of

```
list^.link^.amount
```

Solution 4.3

(i)   *p^.product*

(ii)   *p^.link* is the link field of Timms' order which points to Davis' order, so *p* is assigned the address of Davis' order

(iii) *list^* is the dummy record
       list^.link points to the order following the dummy
       so *list^.link^* is Wilson's record and
       list^.link^.amount has the value 40.

Insertion in the orders list

The orders list is maintained in date order so insertions are made at the end of the list, after the last order on the list and immediately *before* the dummy item. You have already seen (in Section 3) that there is a special technique for insertions at the end of such a list. Figure 4.14 shows a design for this technique.

```
1   create a new order record
2   link it in after the current dummy
3   assign the data for the new order to the dummy item
4   make the list pointer point to the new item
    (which now becomes the dummy item)
```

Figure 4.14

This can be expressed more formally as a module with the input and output parameters shown in Figure 4.15.

insert_at_end

```
list {the external list pointer}
customer_given {customer name}
product_given   {product_name}
amount_given    {quantity on order}
date_given      {date of order}

        Instructions to insert
        the new order at the
        end of the list

list {the list pointer}
```

Figure 4.15

SAQ 4.4

Write down the sequence of Pascal statements to implement the body of the module *insert_at_end* using the design in Figure 4.14.

Solution 4.4

First we need a local pointer variable to refer to the new item to be inserted:

var *new_item : order_ptr;*

Using the pointer variable *new_item*, the body of the Pascal module is as shown in Figure 4.16.

```
    begin
1       new(new_item);
2       new_item^.link := list^.link;
3       list^.link := new_item;
4       list^.customer := customer_given;
5       list^.product := product_given;
6       list^.amount := amount_given;
7       list^.date := date_given;
8       list := new_item
    end
```

Figure 4.16

Line 1 creates a new order record and assigns its address to *new_item*
Lines 2 and 3 link the new order (*new_item^*) in after the dummy order (*list^*)
Lines 4 to 7 assign the order data to the current dummy

Line 8 moves the order pointer to the new order record which is now the dummy.

Deletion from the orders list
In Section 2.3 we presented two modules *timedelete* and *sourcedelete* for deletions from a linked sequence. The former was for use when the item to be deleted was defined by its keyfield and the latter when it was determined by a nonkeyfield. Similar routines can be applied to our list of unfulfilled orders. Suppose we are given the name of a product and wish to delete the first order for this product (if any) from the orders list. A suitable process to perform this deletion can be modelled on the *sourcedelete* module of Figure 2.34.

We shall not pursue the implementation of deletion any further at this point but you will be asked to do something very similar in your practical activity which is the subject of Section 5. You now have all the linked list processing tools necessary to tackle this activity.

4.4 Summary of section

The Pascal implementation of a pointer variable and operations on pointer variables are described. The type definition of a Pascal pointer includes a specification of the type of variable to which the pointer may point. Any attempt to assign to a pointer variable the address of an object of the wrong type is an error which is detected and reported by the Pascal system.

The *getspace* module is implemented by the Pascal procedure *new*. The module *freespace* is implemented by a Pascal procedure *dispose*.

Two problems can arise when processing dynamic variables: *garbage* is created when the only copy of the address of an object is overwritten; a *dangling reference* is created when a pointer variable contains the address of an object which no longer exists because the space allocated to it has been released. Special care is needed to avoid these problems.

The printing of a list of names stored as a linked sequence is presented as an exercise in the use of Pascal pointers.

The unfulfilled orders list from the previous section provides a further example of an application of pointers and operations on them.

5 *Practical exercise*

5.1 Introduction

In this practical activity, you will apply programming techniques for handling linked lists. Your work in this activity will be to write and run a program to perform another operation on the same linked list of orders that we have used in the undelivered orders problem of Section 3.

5.2 The problem

When the warehouse company is informed that a certain product is no longer manufactured, a letter is to be sent to each customer on the list who has ordered that product and the appropriate order is to be deleted from the list. The total quantity of this deleted product on the list is to be computed and written out. The revised list of orders is to be tabulated.

In order to do this exercise you will have to copy the following files from volume **B4:** onto your user disk.

> **B4:UCANCEL.CODE**
> **B4:PCANCEL.TEXT**

The unit **ucancel** provided for your use contains the **type** definitions for the list of order records and the procedures which your program will invoke. The **interface** section of **ucancel** is shown in Figure 5.1. This shows the declarations which have been made for you.

Your task
Your task is to develop and test the program *cancel* given in the program template **PCANCEL**, so that it will carry out the actions specified below.

(i) Invoke *createlist* to initialize the list of orders.

(ii) Invoke *listorders* to tabulate the initial state of the list of orders.

(iii) Invoke *deleteorder* to
(a) Prompt the user to type the name of the product to be deleted and read in this name.
(b) Process the list of orders, invoking *letter* whenever the order is for the named product, accumulating the quantity of cancelled product, deleting the order and disposing of the deleted record.
(c) Write out the total quantity of cancelled product.

(iv) Invoke *listorders* to tabulate the revised list of orders.

Some points to note

1 The pointer *start* and the record structure *ordertype* have been declared for you. They must not be declared again.

2 The procedure *createlist* initializes the *orderlist* and the pointer variable *start*. Its purpose is to create a list of orders, starting with a dummy order pointed to by *start*. The link field in the last order record points back to the dummy record.

3 The procedure *listorders* will display the current state of the orders list on your screen. Its purpose is to help you to test your program. *listorders* has one parameter—the pointer to the first (dummy) order record.

4 The procedure *letter* has one parameter which is the pointer to the record containing the order concerned. The procedure uses the data in the record: the

```
unit ucancel;
interface
type order_ptr = ^ordertype;
     ordertype = record
                    customer : string[20];   {customer name}
                    product  : string[20];   {name of product}
                    amount   : integer;      {quantity on order}
                    date     : string[8];    {date yy/mm/dd}
                    link     : order_ptr     {reference to next record}
                 end;
procedure createlist (var start: order_ptr);
{initialize order list, start points to it}
procedure listorders (start: order_ptr);
{list orders on the back orders list}
procedure letter (p: order_ptr);
{write letter for order record referred to by p}
```

Figure 5.1

customer name, the product name, the quantity and the date of the order.

The letter produced will look like the one in Figure 5.2.

The program template provided for you is listed in Figure 5.3. You will see that you have to implement only one procedure—*deleteorder*.

It is very easy, when typing at the keyboard, to input a string value whose characters are in the wrong case (e.g. lower case when they should be in upper case) or have leading and/or trailing spaces. When this happens it may be the case that your program expects one thing and you have (inadvertently) given it another. Such 'errors' are difficult to spot, so take care!

Before you use the computer, ensure that the variable names you use agree with the variables declared for you in the **unit** as given in Figure 5.1.

You will know from previous experience that after entering your *cancel* program into the computer and correcting any errors in syntax it may still not execute correctly. There may be runtime errors to correct. If so, consider carefully how to trace the program's actions. Perhaps you need to write out the values of records referred to by *start* and *current_order* at strategic points in the program (but remember that you cannot write out a pointer value). One of the most useful aids to debugging a program which uses pointers is to trace its actions by hand, drawing boxes connected by arrows to show the changing values of pointers.

Testing your program
Test what happens when you delete a product. (Note that the names of the products are all in capital letters.) There are three aspects to check:

(i) Does your program print letters to the right customers? You can see who these are from the initial tabulation produced by *listorders*.

(ii) Does the quantity of cancelled product, which your program has written out, agree with your expectation from the initial tabulation?

(iii) Have the correct orders been deleted from the list in the final tabulation?

Does your program behave correctly if you try to delete a non-existent product from the list?

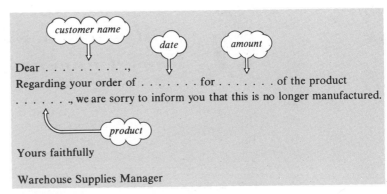

Dear . . . .,
Regarding your order of . . . . . . for . . . . . . of the product
. . . ., we are sorry to inform you that this is no longer manufactured.

Yours faithfully

Warehouse Supplies Manager

Figure 5.2

```
program cancel;
uses {$u ucancel.code}ucancel;
var
    start: order_ptr;
procedure deleteorder;
{PLEASE COMPLETE—declarations of local variables required by
                                                    deleteorder}
begin
    {PLEASE COMPLETE—body of procedure deleteorder}
end;
begin
    createlist(start);
    listorders(start);
    deleteorder;
    listorders(start)
end {of program cancel}.
```

Figure 5.3 *The program template PCANCEL*

When you have finished testing your program, save it for future use.

5.3 Summary of section

In this section you have carried out a substantial piece of practical work involving the application of Pascal programming techniques for manipulating a linked list.

Implementation of the *cancel* procedure involves searching a linked sequence representing the unfulfilled orders list to locate an item containing an order for a specified product and then deleting that order from the list. Deletion of an item from a linked list requires the link field of the preceding item to be changed.

Tracing the execution of a program to detect errors in the processing of pointers is complicated by the fact that pointer values cannot be printed and even if they could they would be meaningless to the programmer. Actions can be traced by printing, at strategic points, the values of the items to which the pointer variables point.

6 Epilogue: Contiguous storage or linked representation?

In program design it is always a good policy to work in terms of the abstract data structure (e.g. the sequence of orders in this unit) as far as possible before committing oneself to a particular representation (either contiguous storage or linked representation in this case). There comes a stage, however, when refinement can be taken no further without including details of the representation.

It is usually the case that there is a choice of representations. In this unit we chose the linked representation based on pointer variables. We could have chosen the contiguous representation of the previous unit. How should such a choice be made? We begin by identifying those parts of the design where it is necessary to know the details of the representation. Then we can consider the advantages and disadvantages of the different possible representations for these parts of the design. In the list of orders problem there are three significant operations which require this knowledge:

(i) Moving from one record to the next, in the searching process.

(ii) Deleting a record for an unfulfilled order that is cancelled.

(iii) Inserting a record for a new unfulfilled order.

(In fact the design of any operation where the list has to be accessed or updated requires the details of the chosen representation to be known.)

A comparison of the linked and the contiguous representations, for these three operations, reveals the following:

(i) In going from one record to the next, the *contiguous* representation requires the index of the *current record* to be incremented by one, whereas the *linked* representation requires a value to be extracted from a link field to determine the next record in sequence. In practice, both methods are quick and easy to use.

(ii) As far as the deletion of a record is concerned, the *linked* representation wins hands down in terms of computer speed. There are only a few pointers to be updated in the linked representation, no matter how long the list might be. You should compare this with the possibility of having to move a significant number of records (on average, half the unfulfilled order list) to close the gap in the *contiguous* representation. This benefit, in speed of processing, of the *linked* representation over the *contiguous* representation, has to be weighed against the additional storage required (for the link fields) and the slight increase in complexity of the final design.

(iii) Additions are made to the end of the unfulfilled order list. Identifying the end of the list precisely is the major problem with the *linked* representation. However, the introduction of the dummy enabled a useful device to be employed. This requires three pointers to be updated, whereas the *contiguous* representation requires only that the value of the size of the list be changed. So here the advantage lies with the *contiguous* representation, both in speed and simplicity of design. Our device avoided having to search through the whole list to find the last record, so that the speed of processing and addition, when using the *linked* representation, does not depend on the length of the unfulfilled order list (as it does, with the *contiguous* representation, in the case of deletions).

On balance, the *linked* representation wins the day in terms of overall speed of execution (if we assume equal numbers of deletions and additions, on average) simply on account of the excessive demands of the *contiguous* representation for deletions. Of course, this may not be a significant saving for short lists and the benefits of simpler programs (easy to design and maintain) may be worth the price. Needless to say, the choice is never obvious. Indeed, we could have presented alternative processes for deletions in the *contiguous* representation which are more efficient. But our aim here is simply to present some of the issues which have to be considered in the design of real programs.

Solutions to exercises

Solution 2.1 _____
The sequence is shown opposite.

Solution 2.2 _____
```
1    set count to zero
2    set current to s {point to dummy}
3    loop while current^.link < > s
4.1      increase count by 1
4.2      set current to current^.link
5    loopend
```

Solution 2.3 _____
```
1    set current to s {point to dummy}
2    set current to current^.link
             {point to first item after dummy}
3    set name to current^.data
             {retrieve data from current item}
```

Steps 1 and 2 could be combined:

```
1    set current to s^.link
             {point to first item after dummy}
```

Solution 2.4 _____
(i)   (17.30, Belfast)
(ii) (17.05, Glasgow)
(iii) (17.45, Dublin)
(iv) (? ?, Edinburgh)—values in dummy
      item.

Solution 2.5 _____
The pointer value returned by *keysearch2*
would be the address of the item preceding
the item with time field equal to *timegiven*

Solution 2.6 _____
Shown opposite.

Solution 2.7 _____
The operations timedelete and sourcedelete
change the time field and the source field,
respectively, in the dummy item but the
actual values stored in the dummy item
have significance only while the search is in
progress. See overleaf.

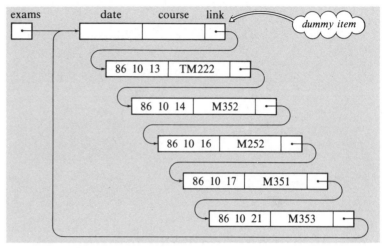

For Solution 2.1

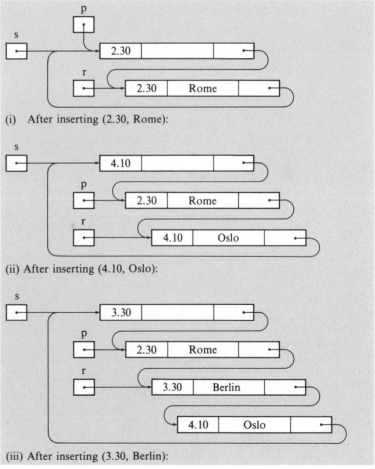

(i)   After inserting (2.30, Rome):

(ii) After inserting (4.10, Oslo):

(iii) After inserting (3.30, Berlin):

For Solution 2.6

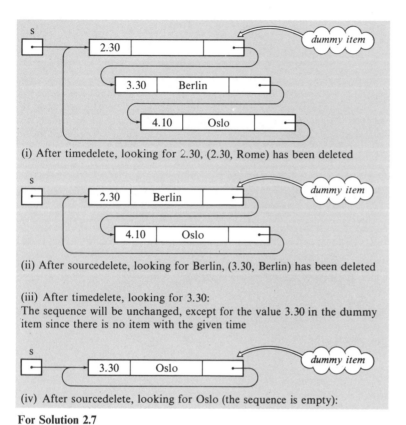

(i) After timedelete, looking for 2.30, (2.30, Rome) has been deleted

(ii) After sourcedelete, looking for Berlin, (3.30, Berlin) has been deleted

(iii) After timedelete, looking for 3.30:
The sequence will be unchanged, except for the value 3.30 in the dummy item since there is no item with the given time

(iv) After sourcedelete, looking for Oslo (the sequence is empty):

For Solution 2.7

Solution 3.1

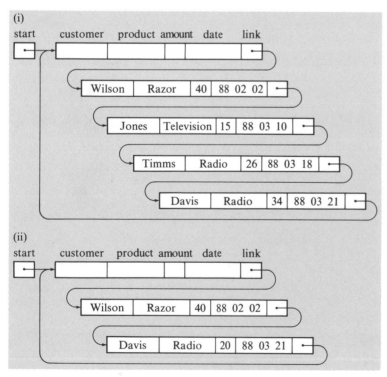

For Solution 3.1

Solution 2.8

(i)

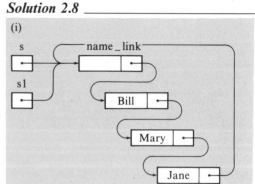

Solution continues on facing page.

Solution 4.1(a)

The refinement of step 1 is:

1.1 set current to point to item to which the link field of the dummy item points

This is expressed formally in Pascal as

current := start^.link

Solution 4.1(b)

writeln(current^.info:10)

Solution 4.1(c)

The address of the next item is stored in the link field of the current item so the refinement is:

set current to current^.link

which is expressed formally in Pascal as:

current := current^.link

Solution 4.1(d)

```
while current < > nil do
  begin
    writeln(current^.info:10);
    current := current^.link
  end
```

(ii)

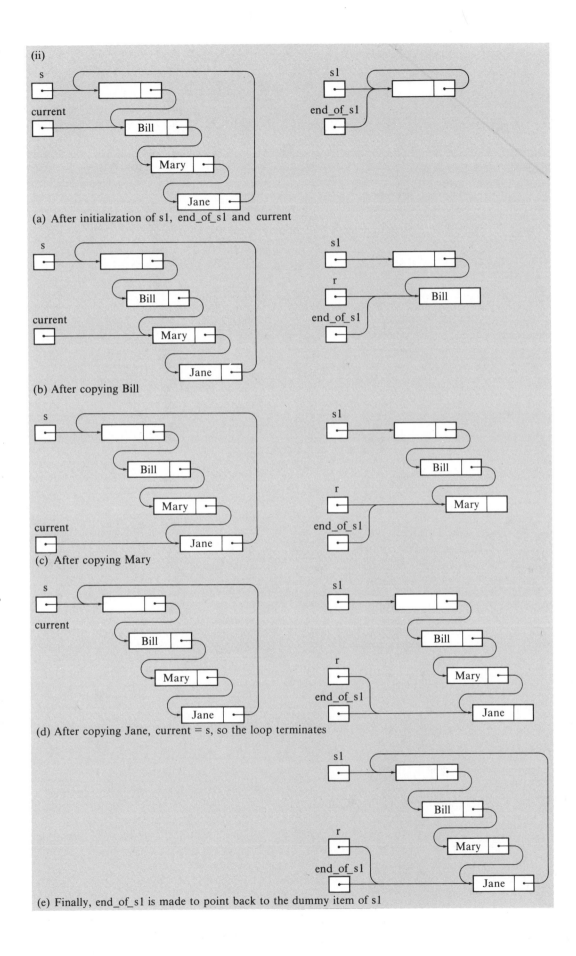

(a) After initialization of s1, end_of_s1 and current

(b) After copying Bill

(c) After copying Mary

(d) After copying Jane, current = s, so the loop terminates

(e) Finally, end_of_s1 is made to point back to the dummy item of s1